AN OPEN DOOR.

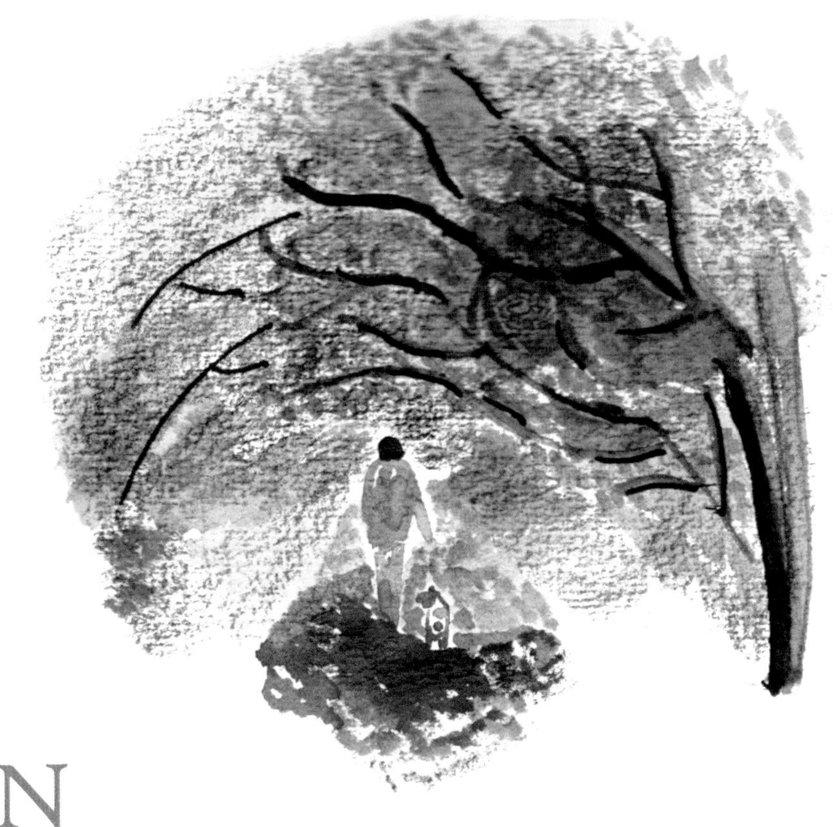

AN INVITATION *to* ENTER IN

MIKE DIXON

WestBow Press books may be ordered through booksellers or by contacting:

WestBow Press
A Division of Thomas Nelson & Zondervan
1663 Liberty Drive
Bloomington, IN 47403
www.westbowpress.com
844-714-3454

ISBN: 979-8-3850-0611-3 (sc)
ISBN: 979-8-3850-0610-6 (e)

Library of Congress Control Number: 2023916296

Print information available on the last page.

WestBow Press rev. date: 10/03/2023

DEDICATION...

This book has been written for all those folks who need a bit of help, support and encouragement through those dark stormy nights of the mind when you can feel so alone.

I would especially like to thank my daughter, Gem, her husband Tim, and my two grandsons Joe and Ben for all their wonderful help, love and encouragement along the way, especially with spelling and punctuation, it's amazing what an 8 and 6-year-old can teach you. I truly want to thank and praise my wife, Gail, my love, my lifelong partner and best friend, my better half who despite all she is going through is a great help, an inspiration and a wonderful support to me, always.

CONTENTS

PREFACE.

Life comes with good times, mediocre times and bad times, just as the writer of Ecclesiastes says in chapter 3, 'A Time for Everything'. For me this has been a time to cry out to the Lord, a time to break down and cry, a time to pour out my heart, a time to pray and a time to stand in faith, a faith that has been shook, rocked and shaken.

Peter found himself not only out at sea in the middle of a storm but walking across the waves of that storm-tossed sea until, through fear, he began to sink into those waves. Peter looked to his Lord and cried out. Help me Lord, Help. There are times when we too need to do as Peter did and cry out for the Lord's help.

Covid 19 was just beginning to appear, 2019 was drawing to a close and 2020 was about to begin. A storm was blowing hard against our life and it appeared determined to sink us. Without the Lords and my family's help I certainly would have sunk.

For my family, my wife and I this has been a very dark, scary and upsetting time that we have walked. The Lord has encouraged me, strengthened me, upheld me and lifted me up, time and time again.

When the person you love dearly becomes very poorly it is hard, to say the least, to see them struggling and unwell. When that illness becomes chronic and no matter how much you pray, the situation deepens and intensifies whilst the person you are willing to get better slips further and further away, it can certainly feel as if the darkness is smothering you. With lockdown in full swing and hospitals stretched to the limit, under the restrictions imposed through the Covid-19 Pandemic, help from the medical profession seemed to be impossible to access. I watched as the woman I love lost half her body weight, eating and drinking were causing her so much pain that she finally stopped doing either for two whole days. We had prayed and prayed and prayed, not just for those two days but for months and months before that, calling out to our Lord, fighting the good fight, declaring the truth and giving thanks, constantly. My wife was fading before my very eye's and I felt heartbroken and helpless to help her. I felt as if, just like Peter, I too was sinking into those storm-tossed waves that were crashing against us. As I lay on my bed one very dark night in the middle of winter, I remember looking out the bedroom window and all I could see was fold upon fold of deep deep darkness. The icy-cold, fear-filled, fingers of that darkness felt as though they were wrapping themselves all around my heart and mind, squeezing together tighter and tighter, but then my eye caught the twinkling light of a tiny star and at that moment I could feel the warmth of hope rising up within me. Jesus is the Light of The World and in Him is Life.

Then the Lord stepped in and He made a way possible.

The content of this book was mainly written down in pencil during the winter of 2019 - 20 and then tweaked throughout 2021/22/23. The individual pages that go together to make this book are a record, mainly, of what I believe to have been, much-needed encouragements from the Lord for myself, through a very hard time. Encouragements to seek Him, sit with Him and listen to Him. I have taken, what is for me, the bold step of compiling them into a book format in the hope that they may be of help to others. I hope as you read and interact with the different titles, throughout this book, that they may also help you come through your own storm and grow in your relationship with the Father which brings you closer to Him and stronger in your walk with God.

As I sit and write these words down we are very definitely still passing through the Storm, the Good News is Jesus is in the boat with us [He will never leave us or forsake us] and we have a destination, a hope and a promise to hold onto, His Word. Above all else, if you have found yourself in a dark situation, then look to God, look to the Author and Finisher of your faith. Look to Him. Strengthen and encourage yourself in the Word. As it says in Hebrews 11 v 1, Faith is the assurance of things hoped for, the conviction of things not yet seen.

After falling on my knees and crying out for the Lord's help, He did, by healing? We are still in the process of that one. By restoring us? Again I believe we are also still in the process of that one too. What I believe He did was to set before us an open door of opportunity to be taught by him, just as he did with the crowds that gathered to Him. He taught them, fed them, and healed them. As I pressed in to help and encourage my wife through this terrible time that she was going through, I also needed to strengthen and encourage myself just as David did at Ziklag. If you have found yourself in a similar position then I would encourage you to sit before him and feed at the Lord's table. Strengthen and encourage yourself in the Word.

INTRODUCTION.

An Open Door.

Revelation 3 verse 8. "I know your works. Behold, I have set before you an open door, which no one is able to shut. I know that you have but little power, and yet you have kept my word and have not denied my name."

The Lord sets before us opportunities, open doors for us to walk through and enter into a new depth of relationship with him, especially at times when we have but little strength of our own and find ourselves down on our knees calling out to him, the Author and Perfector of our faith.

I wrote this book during a very dark, difficult and trying time of my life with a desire in my heart. A desire to help others who also may be going through storms of their own and perhaps feeling a little lost at sea. As you delve into the pages of this book you will encounter 50 different headings, encouragements that the Lord walked me through as he helped me stand against the storm-tossed waves that were crashing against us. I hope as you read through and engage with each of the headings that they will encourage, strengthen, and help to draw you into a deeper relationship with the Lord. Each separate title will walk you through sections of the Bible and give you food for thought. At the end of each reading is a Gateway section, consisting of three questions, invitations for you to connect with the Triune God, Father, Son and Holy Spirit.

THE GATEWAYS.

The Gateways section, which follows at the end of every one of the titles in this book, is there for you. They are an opportunity and an invitation for you to build on your own personal relationship with God. They are an invitation for you to interact with God the Father, God the Son and God the Holy Spirit. I would encourage and urge you to approach these times with a journal, a pen and a willingness to be open to the things of God. Having that pen and paper [actually for me that pen was a pencil] is where the material for this book was initially written down in the first place, gleaned and gathered together out of my personal time with my Father. God is community or family-centred, He is after all the three-in-one, triune God, and he longs for us to join with Him and become part of His family, His close family. Not as some long distant, hardly heard from relation, but as someone who is present, right there, right with you, right in the middle of all that is going on in your life. Take time as you use this section to talk to God, one to one, and then take time to listen for His voice, His prompting, as He responds to you His child. Step through those Gateways and spend time in His presence to see all that He has waiting for you. Expect God to speak to you, after all, His Word says "Call to me and I will answer you." Jeremiah 33 v 3.

I

ALWAYS TRUE.

And you, God, have done what you promised
for you are always true to your word.
Nehemiah 9 v 8 NLT.

Nehemiah 9 v 7 [1]...You are the Lord God who chose Abram and brought him from Ur of the Chaldeans and renamed him, Abraham.

Nehemiah 9 v 8 [1]..When he had proved himself faithful you made a covenant with him to give him and his descendants the Land of .....[Place here God's revealed/spoken promise/Word given to you personally, here.}

and you [God] have done what you promised for you are always true to your word.

God is *ALWAYS TRUE TO HIS WORD.*

....

In the depths of the darkest night, the star is shining, [Italics mine}, and the darkness cannot overcome it.

John 1 v 5 [2.]

The starlight shines brightly twinkling with joy, and the thick dark of the night presses in all around upon the Light. Our focus can either be upon the depths of the darkness or on the Twinkling Light.

....

There are times when things can appear terribly dark and terribly frightening, everything pressing in upon us. It can be heartrendingly painful; how can we possibly go on, how do I continue? David went through just such a time as this at Ziklag in 1 Samuel 30.

After fighting, battles of their own, David and his men return home to find total devastation. Davids's two wives, Ahinoam and Abigail were gone. His family, his whole household, his possessions, everything he had that he held dear, all of it was gone. All of his men's wives, families and belongings were also gone. They had been taken into captivity by an enemy that had completely burned their homes and the whole of Ziklag to the ground. Everything was gone. David and his men, his mighty battle-hardened men of war, broke down, brokenhearted, pouring out their pain and grief collectively. These battle-hardened men of war then turned on David himself, blaming him for their suffering, pain and loss, they even talked about stoning him. How do I go on, how do I get through this, and how do I move forward? David's response, he chose to call upon the Lord, he chose to strengthen and encourage himself in God, his Lord as we can read in 1 Samuel 30 v 6 [3]. David was greatly distressed, for the people spoke of stoning him, because all the people were bitter in soul, each for his sons and daughters. But David chose to strengthen himself in the Lord his God.

Sometimes we too can find ourselves unable to see the answer, the truth or the way forward, because of the pain and confusion within our hearts, that is staring us in the eye, pressing in upon us. Just like David whose eyes were filled with what he was looking at, the smouldering remains of his life - his home, Ziklag, that lay before him. David's ears were filled with the cries of his hurting men. In times of trouble, we need to follow his example by strengthening and encouraging ourselves in the Lord. To look to God and to turn our eyes towards our Lord by turning away from the problem and focusing upon God. In v8 we see how David then inquired of the Lord. He asks God "What do I do? I know what to do, pursue the enemy. But Lord, do I do this, is it the right thing to do? Will we win?"

There are times when, just like David, you know what you are supposed to do, you know what the next step to take is, you know what you need to do right now at this moment, but "Lord is it the right step, how do I go about doing it?" This was one of David's strengths and something that we can learn from him. When he was in trouble and in need he sought the Lord, he asked God, he inquired of him. David would ask his Lord the King, he would seek God's way, God's answer. He is my leader my Helper in times of trouble, He is my guide and what's more, He will answer. John 16 v 24 [4] says "Ask and you will receive." In 1 Samuel 30 v 8 [5] David asked God, "Shall I pursue, shall I win?" ESV. In the very same verse, God answered him and gave him that direction that he needed. He told him what to do. "Pursue: for you shall surely overtake them and without fail recover all." What a Hallelujah, "Thank you God" moment that must have been for David! You shall surely, certainly, overtake them and without fail, most definitely, recover all, get everyone and everything back. The one who is always true does not tell lies, who speaks life, has just given David the green light to do what was already in his heart. So without further ado off goes David to do precisely that. To get back everyone and everything the enemy had stolen away from him and his men. And he did, he recovered all.

In 1 Samuel 30 v 17-19 [6] We can read in v17, David smote the enemy... he slaughtered them, utterly destroyed them, and sent them running.

In v18 we see that David recovered all… Just as God had said to him, He was true to his word. Always True.

In v19 it goes on to say that nothing was missing small or great. All, just as the Lord had said, was recovered.

No matter how dark things become, how bruised we may be feeling, the light of God's truth, the star is always accessible and always shining.

Matthew 12 v 20 [7] "A bruised reed he will not break and a faintly smouldering wick he will not quench until he brings justice to victory." Isaiah 42 v 3 [8] says that He will, *faithfully* bring forth justice. Here is a little breakdown of this verse and the meaning behind some of the words in Matthew 12 v 20.

Justice - Krisis - Strongs G2920 [9], a separating /separation. Separating truth from lies, good from evil, light from the darkness. A just cause. Shall have force of right.

Truth wins. Light wins. Darkness cannot overcome it.

Lead/Bring - ekballo - Strongs G1544 [10], Force overcoming an opposing force. To cause a thing to move straight on to its intended goal.

Victory - Nikos - Strongs G3534 [11], Utterly vanquish. Death is swallowed up in victory.

No matter how dark the night may be, look to God He is the light and He is always true. In him, we have the victory.

The Gateways

Q1. How do you feel or respond to the statement in Nehemiah 9v8 [12] "He is always true!" Do you see this statement as true or do you question it? Ask the Holy Spirit to know the Truth. If you are questioning it, then ask the Holy Spirit to help you see the truth. Is there a blockage/hurt or something in your past that has caused this? Journal his reply and anything that he may reveal to you.

Q2. Are there areas in your life where you are dealing with real emotional pain, hurt and confusion? If so take time to identify them with the Holy Spirit's help and then bring them to the Lord, the answer may already be in your heart. Ask the Holy Spirit to show you the way forward through this time of heartache and pain.

Q3. Let the Holy Spirit guide and direct you in how to act and how to respond, don't let the circumstances govern you. Allow the Holy Spirit to recall to your remembrance the Word of God, the truth, the answer as His way is Always True.

2

A NEW YEAR A NEW PERSPECTIVE?

Sorrow and sighing shall flee away.
Isaiah 35 v 10[1] ESV.

Have you ever been there, New Year, with that heartfelt determination to change something about your life such as lose weight, give something up, or perhaps do that certain something in particular? New Year's resolutions are one of those things that are quickly thought of, quickly proclaimed and then just as quickly they become part of ancient history - past and gone but rarely carried out.

Isaiah 43 v 19[2] says "Behold, I am doing a new thing, now it springs forth do you not perceive it? I will make a way in the wilderness and rivers in the desert". When God says He is going to do something, He does it.

In order for us to gain a new perspective, a new outlook, first of all, we need to see that change is necessary. Isaiah 43 v 19 begins with Behold, the word behold means SEE, not just catch a glimpse of but, to see in-depth something marvellous and wonderful which I AM doing, who is doing you or God? Well in a sense it is both of us, God is the one who is actually doing the something and bringing it to our attention but our part in the whole process is to respond to Him, looking, seeing and then acting. Walking forwards as God makes a way in a wilderness that is blossoming, blooming and bursting forth with fragrant growth.

Isaiah 43 comes after the description of a beautiful flowering wilderness, an oasis laid out and described in Isaiah 35. The thing to be seen here however is that Isaiah 35 comes after Isaiah 34 and Isaiah 34 is a description of a dark wilderness that is full of scary frightening things. Isaiah 34 then becomes Isaiah 35, it is not another land or some other separate place entirely, it is the same wilderness, the same land but the dark scary land has now changed and blossomed into somewhere that is beautiful and refreshing an Oasis from which others, in turn, that pass that way, can draw deeply from and be refreshed. Our lives will continue to change, to grow, to spring forth with new life as we walk forwards with God and accept that there is a need to change to cast off the old ways and move out into the new. This process of change takes time, time spent in the company of the Father. Time spent receiving guidance and direction for our lives on a daily moment-by-moment basis as well as all that we need for our longer-term future, all of which comes through the depth of relationship that we have with the Holy Spirit, Jesus Christ the Son and our Father God.

Change with God will involve removing the dark unpalatable things that have been part of our lives in order to release new fragrant growth, the Cedar, Box, Pine and the Rose. Fragrance to God that is both pleasing and acceptable, and will invigorate and refresh not just ourselves but also those that come our way and leave our company refreshed and nourished. God is not about a New Years' Resolution but a New You.

The question mark over the title New Perspective at the head of this page is Can we SEE the need to change, the need to grow. Can we see the direction in which we must go or as God says **Can We Perceive It?**

The Gateways

1. Read both Isaiah 34 and Isaiah 35. Is the Holy Spirit identifying areas within your life that others may find scary, offensive or upsetting and would not be pleasing or acceptable to God.

2. Do those that come your way leave your company, nourished and refreshed or not.

3. What New thing is God raising up in front of you to see, can you perceive it, if so then acknowledge and act upon it. If not ask for the Lord's help to See. To open your eyes to that which he is doing and wants you to be part of.

3

MORNING GLORY.

For his anger is but for a moment and his favour lasts a lifetime. Weeping may tarry for the night but joy comes with the morning.

Psalm 30 v 5[1] ESV.

A number of years ago we stayed at a B&B with some friends. The landlord asked us what we would like for breakfast and included in the list was Morning Glory. "You see," he said, "Morning Glory needs to be prepared the night before." Morning glory he explained was a mixture of chopped and diced dried fruits and nuts, left overnight, in a bowl of porridge oats soaked in milk. It was then served hot in the morning and drizzled with honey. "Yes please," we said and it was delicious. Morning glory is still part of our diet and it is something that warms, nourishes and feeds our bodies most mornings.

John 21 v 4-14[2]. is a record of a different kind of Morning Glory. After a long, tiring, fruitless night fishing, the empty nets are drawn up into the boat for the last time. Just as the morning sun rises up across the waters of Lake Galilee, a call sounded out from the shore across to the fishermen's ears."Have you any fish?" "No," was their reply. "Cast out your nets on the right side and you will find some." In the Hebrews world, the right side or the right hand is the one that receives, that takes hold of and denotes taking ownership or possession of.

Even though the fishermen, who had been up all night, were probably tired, aching, downcast and ready for home they responded positively, unfurled their nets and cast them out just as they had been prompted. As a result of listening and acting upon what they had heard, their catch of fish was an amazing, bountiful blessing from the Lord, which they were unable to haul in because of the multitude of fish. However, the greatest gift they would receive that morning was about to come their way; an invitation to breakfast. "Come have breakfast with me." John 21 v 12-13[3] *Come dine with me come eat., feast on that which I have already prepared for you.* That simple meal by the lake was drizzled with the Holy Spirit. Jesus Christ, the risen Living God, had prepared nourishment for his friends and he was waiting to serve them personally. The invitation had gone out for them to come and have breakfast, morning glory with their Lord.

Just a few nights previous to this moment by the lake Jesus had agonised through the night in the Garden of Gethsemane, preparing future nourishment for us His family. It even caused him to sweat blood. He agonised as He went to and hung on a cross in the darkness, delivered into a dark sealed tomb where Morning Glory, Jesus, burst forth from death to life, victory! With that invitation to come dine with Him written right through his life - his death - his resurrection, this is my body broken for you. *Feast upon my goodness. Feast upon me, upon all that I have done for you and receive.*

The Lord has already prepared for us all that we need, sometimes however the night that we are passing through can feel long, dark and empty. Full of disappointment, full of discouragement, full of fear and anxiety, full of emptiness. "Now what will I eat? How will I live? I have nothing." Jesus, however, has prepared and the Holy Spirit is ready to fill up your nets abundantly. Dine with Him this morning, and spend time in His company. Allow the Holy Spirit to drizzle you with morning glory and receive His nourishment, all that you need for your day ahead.

The Gateways

1. As Peter feasted on that which the Lord had prepared for him by the lake, there came a tough heart-searching question, "Do you love Me?" It was repeated two more times. This in turn was followed by the direction for his life," Feed My Sheep." As you feast on this scripture in John 21 v 15-17[4], is God speaking to you about His will for your life? Write down in your journal all that He has to say to you.

2. Do you take time to enjoy your Morning Glory with the Lord? Time to sit down and digest what has been laid on the table before you? Or do you grab something to go and rush past the breakfast table? Perhaps you don't even stop at the breakfast table, and go straight on into your day without any nourishment at all. Why do you think it's important to start the day with the Lord? Peter cast out his nets in the morning.

3. Morning Glory was prepared the night before so as to be ready for the morning. Sunrise. God is always at work in us and never leaves us. Do you feel as if you are toiling through the night, fruitlessly? Are you pulling in your nets empty for the last time? This is exactly when Jesus spoke and urged that the nets be cast out in a certain way. I urge you to listen, this day, for the Lord's voice - for His direction. Be prepared to receive and act.

4

THE HONKING OF THE GEESE.

For He himself has said I will never leave you nor forsake you.
Hebrews. 13 v 5[1] NKJV.

The Geese, Barnacle Geese, have just flown over our house stretched out across the sky in their V-shaped formations. I know this because I heard them fly over our rooftop, honking, trumpeting or bugling out loud to one another. Thousands come here to overwinter every year, great flocks of them gathering in the fields all around my home. They may well be all around me but the only way to get to know and recognise them is by spending time in their presence, by seeing - observing and listening to them. The more time you take to do this the better you become at differentiating between breeds of Geese and the easier it becomes to recognise them by their call, appearance or behaviour.

You can actually hear the geese from a long way off, coming on their way, calling out one to another "Here I am, Here I am, right with you right with you," as they fly high overhead in their tight formations held together in place by a constant flow of communication.

"Here I am, right with you, this way," a constant, constant, uninterrupted flow of communication is passed on from one to another. The sound of their calls being carried on the wind right to my ears. Just as the Words of Life are carried to our ears by the Wind of God, the Holy Spirit. Communication.

Jesus as He walked this earth had such a union with His Father, constant communion one to another. Always listening, always seeing what the Father had to say to Him and was showing Him. Jesus also said we could have that same sort of relationship with Him, with the Father and with the Holy Spirit. Constant communion one with another. Communication.

He says Hebrews 13 v 5 that He will never leave us nor forsake us. Always there, always with us, supporting us, encouraging us and directing us, helping us but never leaving us nor forsaking us. Communing with us.

Geese are loyal, steadfast and mate for life they are always connected talking to each other, "Here I am," feeding together, walking together, flying together, sheltering together and raising their family together. God is always with us, sheltering us, feeding us, walking with us, flying high with us, helping to raise us up and to raise our families. Even in the wildest darkest weather, you can still hear the geese honking, calling out one to another here I am, here I am, all through the storm. Even when things look at their darkest, listen for the Father, listen for the still small voice, calling out to you. "Here I am here I am, right with you right with you."

Psalm 50/15[2], Call upon me in the day of trouble, I will deliver you and you shall glorify me.

2Sam22v4[3], I called to the Lord, who is worthy of praise, and have been saved from my enemies.

John 14 v26[4], "But the Helper, The Holy Spirit, whom the Father will send in my name, he will teach you all things and bring to your remembrance all that I have said to you."

Spend time in the company of the Father, Son and Holy Spirit, commune with them, and get to know them, the sound of their voice - appearance and behaviour.

The Gateways

1. John 10 v 3 and 10 v 27 Jesus points out a few times that My Sheep know my voice and follow me. We, me and you, his sheep know His voice.

Getting to know God's voice more intimately comes by spending time with Him, engaging with Him, just as you would with another person. Do you enjoy talking with God or are you unsure what to say? Remember, He is your friend and is longing to have a relationship with you.

Take time to listen to Him as you call out, here I am. Take time to allow the Holy Spirit to minister to you as you seek to grow in wisdom knowledge and understanding of who God is. Take time to listen for that Still Small Voice calling out to you, "Here I Am."

2. There are many instances throughout the Old and New Testaments of God speaking to His People. Take time to study out some of the different ways this happened. Samuel as he walked along a row of brothers, clear guidance on who was to be King, [1 Samuel 16]. Gideon being assured and strengthened in his identity in God, [Judges 6v12]. Moses and the burning bush, taking time to respond, turn aside and see and in doing this God told Moses what he was to do [Exodus 3]. Journal what the Lord reveals to you as you study them.

3. Do you look and listen for God, the Holy Spirit, to speak to you personally and show things to you? If not, ask Him to open your eyes that you might see. Elisha prayed that Gehazi's eyes might be opened and that he might see, [2 Kings 6v17[6],] then it says 'And He Saw". Ask the Lord.

5

FIRST STEPS.

If anyone walks in the day, he does not stumble for he sees the light of this world. John 11 v 9[1] ESV.

When a child is learning to walk we help - we aid - we assist and encourage those first tottering steps to improve, strengthen and become more confident. We don't use our own feet to push obstacles in the child's way that would hinder or unbalance them so that they may fall, that would be unkind and cruel. In the same way Romans 14 v 13[2] is entitled, "Do not cause another to stumble" and goes on to say, "but rather decide never to put a stumbling block or hindrance in the way of a brother." The Bible tells us to think upon what is good, uplifting and encouraging Philippians 4 v 8[3] ESV, or another way you could say this is, to fix your eyes, your thoughts, on the good in any situation. If we are to be a source of encouragement then we need to have our eyes fixed upon our Lord and Saviour, so that we in turn can overflow with God's goodness through our actions and words towards those we meet.

John 10 v 10 warns us that the enemy comes to steal, kill, rob and destroy. We are given a choice, life or death set before us. There is always a choice for us to make whatever the situation may be. However, God gives us the answer to that choice and guides us to choose life Deuteronomy 30 v 19. When someone is in need of help we can choose to be of assistance and help that person. Or we can choose to knock them down with harsh words, a bad attitude, or simply by ignoring them, looking past them and passing by on our way Luke 10 v 31-34. Walking in the dark causes us to stumble, but *if we walk in the light* we do not stumble. Sometimes we can find ourselves in need of help to find the light switch that will dispel the darkness, help to keep us on our feet and aid us to understand, we need help to see our way forward. As children of God, we have been called to be a Light in this dark world. To be a source of life, not death.

Encourage one another, be a sweet aroma, a fragrance of God, don't be cruel, a stink and cause others to stumble in the dark. All too often we can speak harsh words that can cause those around us to stumble, fall and feel crushed with all sense of hope and expectation taken away. We can be dogmatic, harsh judgemental, and uncaring and all of this is carried out in the name of God. Love and understanding are what's needed, without the Love of God we are no more than a clanging gong 1 Corinthians 13v1. Speak life, speak encouragement, speak love. Help those trying to take steps to walk forwards and grow in confidence in who they are in Christ. Help don't hinder, build up don't knock down. Help someone walk forwards in life to take those first tottering steps out of the darkness of the world that enshrouds them, to step forth in light and life. Don't knock their legs right out from under them. Lazarus had died, been wrapped up in death shrouds and placed within a sealed-up tomb. Jesus called him out of the tomb, to rise up and live. Lazarus came out of that tomb fully alive but he needed others to help, roll away the tombstone and unwrap the shrouds of death that still covered him from head to foot. Jesus called for others to come forward and remove those shrouds from his face and body, to assist him and not to hinder him. John 11 v 38-44.

The Gateways

1. Are there shrouds of darkness cloaking your vision? Is The Lord encouraging you to walk forward? Has God called someone else to help you to do this? If so acknowledge that you need that help and accept it gratefully.

2. 1 Thessalonians 5 v 11 calls us to encourage one another and build each other up. Take time to allow the Holy Spirit to recall to your remembrance the times when others have encouraged you. Thank God for those folks who answered that call and didn't just pass you by.

3. Is there someone within your circle that God is lifting up in your heart? Ask the Lord for ways in which you could support or encourage that person. Remember to do it with Love. Remember the first response to helping Lazarus was, "Oh but Lord he stinks".John 11 v 39[4].

6

WHEN GOD CALLS.

Come follow me.

Matthew 4 v 19 NIV

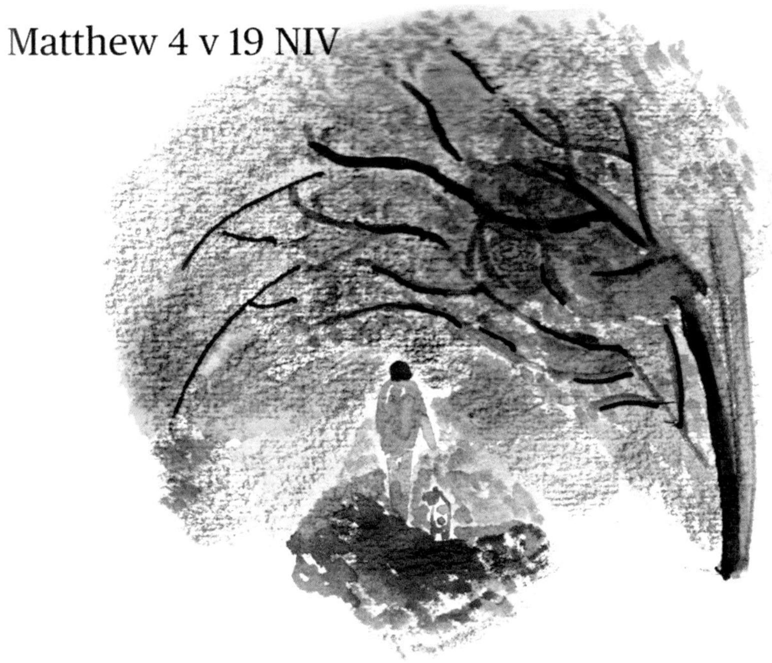

Come follow me.

Matthew 4 v 19 NIV.

God's spoken voice changes things, as can be seen right at the beginning of the bible in Genesis 1 v 3[1]. "And God said "Let there be light" and there was light." He turned darkness into light, and He brought order out of chaos, by speaking. Jesus said "I am the light of the world. Whoever follows me will not walk in darkness, but will have the light of life" John 8 v 12[2]. Light is understanding and understanding removes ignorance - darkness. John 9 v 5[3] says "As long as I am in the world I am the light of the world." In John 11 v9[4] Jesus says "Are there not twelve hours in a day? If anyone walks in the day, he does not stumble, because he sees the light of this world." Walking in the company of Jesus keeps us in the light. Walking without light, in darkness, without understanding, is going to lead to a stumble.

When God calls out to us he is about to do something, things are about to change. Your life, your outlook, and your position with God are about to change. As Jesus walked by the shore of Lake Galilee he called out to some fishermen, "Come follow me" and from that moment on their lives were changed forever. Matthew 4v18 - 22[5].

Jesus spoke to Saul, not face to face, but out of a cloud on the road to Damascus. Saul was marching forward to persecute Christians. Jesus's call changed Saul's life completely. It changed his position, outlook, understanding and mission in life as he became Paul. From the Pharisee Saul, the persecutor of the followers of Christ, to Paul the Apostle, messenger of Jesus Christ. Paul, a person who wrote a major portion of the new testament and became the voice of good news to the Gentiles introducing them to live a life with Christ. Acts 9 v 1 - 22

A little boy named Samuel lay on his bed in the dark and heard his master call his name. Repeatedly he responded by getting up and going to see his earthly master Eli until finally the penny dropped and Eli understood that the voice the little boy was hearing was actually that of his Heavenly Master. The Lord was calling Samuel, Eli having realised, that this was God, instructed him on what to do and how to respond. When He calls ask "What will You say to me?" Samuel did as Eli instructed and he learned an important lesson in how to recognise his Lord's voice. The voice that he would rely on, respond to and be obedient to for the rest of his life. A voice that would one day call him to anoint an unlikely young shepherd boy, David, King. 1 Samuel 3

When God calls, take time to recognise His voice, to see and hear what He is wanting to say to you. His voice doesn't just sound but it also brings light to something. It shines a light on a problem, a question that you need an answer to, the light of understanding on something confusing. Confusion is darkness. Take time to listen for the Master's voice and take time to respond when He breaks into your daily routine. Time to stop and go back over the scripture that has just lifted up off the page in front of your eyes. Time to respond and change, to move into a new life, a new you, a new page, a new day, a new chapter in your life with God.

Take time to listen and respond when God calls you.

The Gateways

1. Take time to read and pray over the scriptures shown above where people have been called by the Lord. Journal what the Holy Spirit is saying to you in each of these stories.

2. Why do you think it is important to respond to the prompting of the Holy Spirit?

3. Is The Lord calling you and leading you in a certain way?

7

WE ARE NOT ALONE.

Jesus answered him if anyone loves me he will keep my word and my father will love him, and we will come to him and make our home with him.

John 14 v 23[1] ESV.

The World is desperate to find alien life; to prove that we are not alone. Whether it's by looking back into the distant past for signs of visitors from another planet. Or looking out into the vastness of space to the countless stars above for evidence of life and an answer to the calling within; the deep, deep desire to not be alone.

Loneliness can be a very dark, isolating and debilitating place in which to live. The world can live in the midst of all that comes with the hustle and bustle of a big, busy city and yet still be very alone.

However, the Bible tells us just the opposite and it is full of evidence that we are not alone. God, Himself tells us in the Bible that He will never leave us and that He will never forsake us Hebrews 13 v 5. That He the Father, the Son and the Holy Spirit dwells within us John 14 v 23-26. All of creation bows to Him, calls to Him and we are part of that creation. That longing to not be alone comes from the deep call that is within us, it is the calling out of our hearts to the Creator, our Father God. His desire is for us to walk through this life in unity and union with Him. Not separate, cut off and alone, but vitally united and connected to our Father by being grafted into His family. God the Father made that possible through His Son, the Lord Jesus Christ. The enemy/darkness desires to keep us separated from the great I Am our Father in Heaven. Separation is cold, isolating and lacking, it is darkness.

Have you ever found yourself in the dark about something? Like you were the isolated one that was in the dark about something going on outside of your understanding? Do you recall just how alone that dark can make you feel? Isolated, separated, disconnected.

We were created to live in union one with another and not as isolated, solitary beings. In Genesis, God took time and effort to first create Adam, on his own, and then to point out by saying, it is not good for man to live alone and He then created woman, Eve. All along it is His desire for us to walk in the garden with Him, to spend quality time in close communion with one another. A garden is full of life and needs light for it to grow, it also needs the loving care and knowledge of a gardener who carefully chooses and selects the plants, where to place them and which plant will go with which. Companion planting, as it is called, promotes good healthy growth and also helps to prevent disease and invasion from unwanted, harmful pests. The cry of the Father today is "Walk with me, don't walk alone in isolation, but walk in companionship with Me." As a Christian I am never alone because I Am is always with me, He is my constant companion.

The Gateways

1. How do you relate to God? As someone or something?

As your close companion or as some distantly unreachable being?

2. Do you see yourself as alone or hand in hand with God?

3. How do you see space? Is it cold, dark and isolating or full of bright twinkling stars reminding us of our Creator and how amazing He is? Take time to look up at the night sky and to look out into the vastness of who He is and give thanks that He chose you to be part of His family, to be His beloved.

8

A CLOVE OF GARLIC.

I came that they may have life and have it abundantly.
John 10 v 10[1] ESV.

As the days shorten and the nights lengthen, before winter comes howling in, is the time to plant garlic out into your garden. It's the time to bury these cloves into the soil from which they will root, and draw their sustenance, causing them to grow and produce a bigger crop of garlic come the summertime harvest. Which in turn, once properly stored, will feed and maintain us through the following winter season to come. Being planted out at the right time allows those cloves of garlic to respond to the cold winter frosts, that cause the individual cloves to split and produce multiple cloves come harvest time.

Once planted we need to safeguard them from pests, such as pigeons and mice that come to uproot and pull them out of the soil. We keep watch over our new planting and l have found one such clove pulled up, carried across the garden, and hidden beneath a piece of wood out of sight. It had been hidden, out of sight in the dark. That clove had still rooted into the ground and produced a shoot. Having found it I returned it to the garlic bed, back to its rightful place in my garden, Luke 15 v 5 - 6. The life within that clove was determined to live and produce the harvest that is held within.

Isaiah 55 v 10 - 11[2] just as we see in these verses, God causes the right conditions to come down upon the ground. In verse 10, "For as the rain and the snow come down from heaven and do not return there but water the earth, making it bring forth and sprout." We see rain and snow mentioned here, but for the garlic clove, the touch of icy cold frost is needed, which God provides. These conditions then cause the earth to bring forth the crop that is buried within the soil. Verse 11, then goes on to point out how God's word works on the same principle and says "So shall my word be that goes out from my mouth; it shall not return to me empty, but it shall accomplish that which I purpose, and shall succeed in the thing for which I sent it". Other versions don't just say accomplish but flourish and prosper. The seed/ life within God's spoken word will produce a harvest. IT HAS TO. It is the power, the purpose, the life force of God himself contained within it and it will bring forth that harvest. Just to confirm it and God also says, as we have just read, "it does not come back void, empty or unfulfilled." It does not come back empty, God's word does not fail.

As we take God's revealed word and plant it within our hearts it is going to produce a harvest. Just like the garlic clove that seed of God's word needs to be planted out at the right time, the time of revelation. We need to receive that word seed and bury it within the soil of our hearts. We then need to care for it, guard it, meditate and think upon it, write it down, journal it and speak it out. That seed word is going to grow within us and multiply as God himself causes that word to grow within our lives. He waters it with the early rain and the latter rain coming down from heaven Deuteronomy 11 v 14. He encourages us to grow.

That word will increase and grow, it may well get swept up in darkness, momentarily carried away with troubles, disappointments, doubts, anxieties and fears. Our God is a good God and He cares for us, recovering us. The life within that seed word is powerful and it will complete that which it has been sown to do, recovered to the garden and bring forth new life. Bursting out and producing a multiple crop of abundant life that is held within it, and as it overflows, will produce food and nourishment not only for ourselves but also for others that God has gathered to us and intends for us to feed. God's word always produces abundant life that overflows and feeds. The Life of Jesus was sown upon a cross where He died in deep darkness. Luke 23 v 44[3], "It was now about the sixth hour, and there was darkness over the whole land until the ninth hour."

His body was laid within a dark tomb yet just as the darkness of the soil cannot contain the life held within a seed, the Living Word of God that is within our Lord burst forth in new Life and fed all those that, gathered to Him and received Him. That same Abundant Life that He held within Him and freely offered to us, came from the one clove of Jesus' life sown, in love, upon a cross for each and every one of us. John 19 v 41. John 10 v 10

The Gateways

1. Can you recognise areas of your life that have received the frosting of winter that in due course have brought forth fruitful growth? If so, take time to thank the Lord for that growth.

2. Take time to ask the Holy Spirit to show you the area where God is wanting to bring new growth into your life.

Journal His response and meditate on it, sowing the seeds of what He reveals to you into your heart. Thank Him for the crop of new life to come.

3. If I want a crop of garlic from my garden I must sow cloves of garlic into my soil. If I want a crop from God's garden I must sow God's Word into my garden, my heart. What are you currently sowing into your heart? What do you watch, listen to, read and spend time with? Whatever seed you are sowing will produce like-kind in your garden. Ask the Holy Spirit to show you what you attend to most and what needs to change, journal His response.

9

IN ORDER TO SEE WE MUST FIRST HEAR.

Having the eyes of your heart enlightened that you may know what is the hope to which he has called you, what are the riches of his glorious inheritance in the saints.

Ephesians 1 v 18[1] ESV.

Genesis 1[2]. "In the beginning. God created the heavens and the earth. The earth was without form and void, and darkness was over the face of the deep. And the Spirit of God was hovering over the face of the waters. And God said,

"Let there be light," and there was light. And God saw that the light was good. And God separated the light from the darkness.

In Genesis 1 v 2 we read how in the beginning there was just darkness and how darkness was over the face of the deep. The first thing to happen is God speaks, "Let there be light" and there was light. For there to be light and for the light to be seen it needed God to speak. Then the world hears the spoken word, "light," and then the world sees light. How often does darkness sit on our faces and we are unable to see the answer, the solution we require? In order to receive revelation [light] upon something, we must first open our ears to hear what God is saying to us. Give attention to what's being said, the darkness of unknowing/ not understanding will shroud our hearts and minds with fears, unbelief, doubts and misconceptions. But as we hear God's voice, the Light of the World, and listen to Him, the layers of darkness are penetrated, pierced by the truth of the true and living word. Those layers are unravelled and peeled back in order to reveal what's been hidden from us, the truth, God's truth through the light of understanding.

As the angel of the Lord calls Ezekiel back to the banks of the river, not to full emersion in the river but to the point and position where he gets to see what lies beyond. The angel of the Lord says, "Son of man have you seen this." Ezekiel 47 v 6[3]. Ezekiel must first hear the spoken word and then respond to the call in order to see what he is being shown. He is first called to come and see. If you want to see what lies beyond, listen. Don't become so hard of hearing that you already think you're fully immersed, there is always more to see. Ephesians 1 v 18 ESV. "Having the eyes of your hearts enlightened, that you may know what is the hope to which he has called you, what are the riches of his glorious inheritance in the saints." Open your ears, your heart, to hear - don't live in the darkness. Jesus died so that the veil would be removed, open your ears and allow the shrouds of darkness to be removed. Lazarus, fully alive in Christ, responded to Jesus's spoken word and walked forward out of a dark tomb. But the shrouds of death that were wrapped all around him had to be removed as well as the covering that was over his face before he could fully receive the light of the Sun on his face.

Don't walk alive in Christ yet shrouded in darkness and unbelief. Ask God to speak to you so that you might "See" and "Behold," something wonderful, something truly amazing, the Light of Life.

The Gateways

1. Invite the Holy Spirit to come and reveal areas of your life that are shrouded with darkness.

Ask the Holy Spirit to pierce this darkness with light, the light of understanding.

2. Is there an area of your walk with God where He is calling you back to the River to gain a deeper understanding of something particular?

Thank him for growth.

3. Mark 8 v 22-26 Jesus leads the blind man out of the town before healing him and restoring his sight. Is the Lord calling you out from an area of your life that is so busy and noisy that it is blinding you to the things of God? Spend time with the Lord and ask Him to help you be still so that you might hear what He has to say to you.

SEATED WITH CHRIST.

For he raised us from the dead along with Christ and seated us with him in the heavenly realms because we are united with Christ Jesus.

Ephesians 2 v 6[1] NLT.

So often we are told, reminded even, that our position is at the feet of Christ. That we are to lay ourselves down at His feet and rightly so. We should come and cast ourselves down at His feet, the Son of God, the living God our Saviour. We choose to lay our lives down to Him, freely, as a living sacrifice and to fully submit - surrender - die to self and acknowledge that it is no longer I that live but Christ that lives in me. Galatians 2 v 20[2], ESV. "I have been crucified with Christ. It is no longer I who live, but Christ who lives in me. And the life I now live in the flesh I live by faith in the Son of God, who loved me and gave himself for me."

How many times do we proclaim that verse, yet out of a "well done me" position? No, to come to this position of a fully laid down life we must first humble ourselves and acknowledge I can't actually do this, die to self, without You Lord, without Your help. I can't lay my life down at Your feet unless You, Lord, help me to die to self. I may well be able to say it, to think it, to want to die to self but the whole process needs God's help, God's loving hand. Once we take this step of faith of moving forwards to a life immersed in God it is God who will complete and perfect our faith. So often we are then encouraged to remain in that position at His feet, to stay there. Yet Ephesians 2 v 6 clearly says we die with Him, Christ, then we are risen up with Him, Christ, to be seated with Him in the heavenly realm. God is the One who is laying us down, raising us up and seating us. Your position is seated with Christ.

You have a seat of your own with your name on it next to Jesus, the Son of God. God himself has prepared a place at His table for you, the family table, His table, Psalm 23 v 5. You are seated with the Son of God because you also are a child of God, an heir apparent. You are not a slave, nor a beggar or an outcast but family; a child of God accepted and seated. So often we can miss what we are or who we are because we listen to lies, slippery smooth-tongued lies of the serpent. "You failure, you good for nothing" or "you brilliant star, you deserve more." Beware of the slippery tongue that can just as easily puff you up, vanity, as knock you down. Listen to the truth, you are "Seated" next to the Risen Christ in the heavenly realm. You are a Child of God full of hope, full of promise, full of life. A life that is full and abundant with an expected end, with a plan and a purpose. Not just any old purpose, but a God-given purpose that is uniquely yours and it's from your Father, your heavenly Father. You have a rich inheritance, so remain seated with Christ in your rightful place. Don't abdicate.

The Gateways

1. Do you believe your Father has taken the time and effort to set or prepare a place just for you at His table? Take time to pray over Psalm 23 v 5 and ask the Holy Spirit to help you see your place at the table.

2. We can refer to being part of God's family as simply meaning we are members of a Church group. Does seeing yourself seated with Christ, or sitting in your seat at the Father Gods' table change this view?

3. Don't forget you are who you are in Christ because of Jesus Christ and all that He has done for us and not because of what we've accomplished ourselves. Take time to give praise and thanks to the Lord for who He is and what He did for you personally. Journal His response to you as you praise Him.

THIS IS THE DAY THAT THE LORD HAS MADE.

This is the day that the Lord has made
let us rejoice and be glad in it.
Psalm 118 v 24[1] ESV.

It's January and it's mid-winter, the days are short and the morning has dawned grey. It's raining and the forecast is for more and strong gale-force winds as well. So what am I going to do with today? Walk around shrouded in grey, remain shut up within my walls, afraid to venture out or smile and let the sunshine in? How? There is none forecast.

Psalm 118 v 24[2] NKJV says "This is the day that the Lord has made, we will rejoice and be glad in it." Choose to be glad choose to rejoice. Isaiah 55 v 10 says the rain comes down and waters the earth and brings forth its crops so shall My word be that goes forth from my mouth.

This is the day that the Lord has made. God is a good God and within the soil of this day, there are to be found crops of God's goodness. Water them with His word, with thanksgiving in our hearts and a song of praise on our lips. His mercies are new every day, great is His faithfulness Lamentations 3 v 20-23. The Bible also tells us Luke 11 v 33-36 about the eye, the lamp of our body - our heart. An eyeful of dark fills our hearts with darkness. An eye that sees light allows light to fill our hearts and minds. Find something good to think about or look upon. That light will spill out into the greyness of the day causing joy. Gladness and health to begin to well up within it. Light nourishes and encourages growth whereas dark causes things to shrivel up and die. Paul, whilst on a ship in the middle of a terrible dark storm, says until all hope of being saved was taken from them but then an angel of the Lord - light - stood beside him and brought hope of promises yet to be fulfilled as well as for instructions on how he and the crew were to be delivered, safe.

On a dark grey, morning look to the Creator of that day, God, and give thanks. Within that darkness, that greyness, we can still focus our eyes on Him. Allowing His light to enter in, allowing thankfulness to overflow and allowing the goodness of God to enter into our day. Look for the simple things to be thankful for because as we give thanks for the little it makes way for the greater to come through. Jesus stood before 5000 men, plus women and children, and in His hands was a small boy's lunch with which to feed them all. The first thing He did was to give thanks for what he had. Give thanks for your daily bread and stand ready with baskets in hand to gather up the abundance of God's goodness released especially on a grey rainy day. Remember, I *will* give thanks, it's an act of will, I *will*, it's a choice, our choice, one we need to choose. To be glad, choose to rejoice. Not an easy thing to do especially when we are in the middle of something dark. Yet praise unlocks chains and destroys the work of the enemy.

The Gateways

1. There are accounts where choosing to rejoice and give thanks changed dark situations - Paul and Silas in prison, {Acts 16 v 16-40}.

Jehoshaphat and the people walking out to battle singing and praising whilst facing overwhelming odds against them. {2 Chronicles 20 v 20-30}.

Read over these accounts and ask the Holy Spirit to recall to your mind times when praising God has changed situations for the better in your own life.

2. Ask God to help you rejoice and to give thanks in a certain awkward situation that you may be encountering at the moment. Praising God in the difficult times takes faith, faith moves mountains.

3. Choosing to give thanks can change your outlook, why not choose today to start keeping a "Thank You" journal, in which you thank the Lord daily for the good things that you experience. Help to make thankfulness part of your daily life filling your eye and your heart with light. Take time to sit with the Lord and write down three things to be thankful for, pray over those three things and then ask the Lord to help you expand them, to add to what you have written and grow in thankfulness. For instance,"Thank you for my Garden." Then expand on it. "Thank you for my Garden, for the birds and the flowers. Thank you that there is always something to see and enjoy." It's amazing how much more you see to be thankful for, just have a go and try it out.

12

STAND ON IT, OR HOW TO RECEIVE SOMETHING GIVEN TO YOU BY GOD.

Every place that the sole of your foot will tread upon
I have given to you, just as I promised to Moses.
Josh 1 v 3 ESV.

In Joshua 1 v 3[1] the Lord speaks to Joshua and tells him. "Every place that the sole of your foot will tread upon l have given to you just as I promised Moses."

Something given to you by God is sealed in a divine promise and that promise is His word. Along with this promise will come God's guidance and instruction on how to receive it in its fulfilment. God had promised to give His people the promised land and here we see God pointing out to Joshua that whatever he places beneath the sole of his foot is his. This action of placing something under the sole of his foot, that which he stands on, denotes ownership.

The greatest demonstration we can see of this was when Jesus himself stood on Satan's head and bruised it, and in the process He took back ownership of the keys to the kingdom.

Have you ever bought a new house, all the legal work is done, the paperwork has been completed, it's the big day and the key has been handed over it's now yours? Time to go and take possession, what does that involve, just a piece of paper, if it is just a piece of property possibly but even then there is more to it than just that.

If this is the place where you are to live then you need to move in and become acquainted with what you've got, explore the rooms that come with your property. Walk through them get to know what is yours, check out your boundaries, and piece by piece get the overall picture of what you have got and what is now yours. As we see it and walk through it we start to fully take ownership/possession of that which we have just received the keys to. I have lived in my present property for over 6 years and there is still one room I have not set foot in as yet, it's the attic above my garage, there is still more for me to take hold of and reveal what's inside what's yet to find or discover.

In Genesis 13 v 14-15/17[2]. The Lord gives Abram land and says, The LORD said to Abram after Lot had separated from him, "Lift up your eyes and look from the place where you are, northward and southward and eastward and westward, for all the land that you see I will give to you and to your offspring forever". Moving on to v 17 God then directs him to, "Arise, walk through the length and the breadth of the land, for I will give it to you." Abram needed to walk through it in order to get to know it and possess it, to walk the length and breadth of it. This is possibly the earliest record of God giving us directions on how to take possession of something that he is giving to us.

As God lifts up a portion of scripture to you, He is giving you, showing you, something that he wants you to know, to take possession of. It's time to lift up your eyes, don't just skim over it but give your full attention to what the Holy Spirit is revealing to you. In looking and seeing we take possession of what is being revealed to us to own. Once we see that which God is showing us, we then need to take time to explore it and possess it. Abram, once he had looked up and seen was directed to walk. We walk through the revelation by exploring the length and breadth of that which is laid in front of us, reading the scripture over and over, meditating upon it and looking deeper into what God is telling us, what He's giving us to own. My eyes have been amazed, and opened, at what is revealed by breaking scriptures down into a word-by-word study and getting a hold of the depth of what is set before you. Just as with my garage attic and what lies within, you can be sure that in due course more will be opened up, The Holy Spirit will reveal more to you that is hidden within that scripture. More for you to take hold of, more to help you grow in your relationship with God, more for you to understand. God is always calling us back to the river Ezekiel 47 v 6 to the point at which we may feel we have become fully immersed in what is to be known at this point, but then The Lord says behold see, own, what I am showing to you, take it, receive it, feed upon it and then go and feed others.

The Gateways

1. Is there a particular scripture, or portion of a scripture, that the Holy Spirit keeps bringing to your mind?

Spend some time reading over it with God. Walk through it again and again, by reading it, asking Him to show you, to open your eyes to All that lies within. Journal all that He shows you.

2. God gave Habakkuk directions about how to deal with a vision that He had given him. Write the vision down so whoever reads it can run with it. As God reveals things to you, write them down, record them, and journal them so that you can go over and over them, as can those that God leads you to share it with.

3. Luke 5 v 4 Describes how Simon [Peter] was commanded to put out into the deep and let down his nets for a catch. Once God has spoken to you through scripture, are you prepared to let down your nets for a catch, into the Deep [the mysteries of God] and expect an awesome catch, something that will feed you? Or have you, just like Simon had, excuses, reasons for not doing so?

13

CAN I BORROW THE PENCIL SHARPENER?

Ask and it will be given to you.
Matthew 7 v 7[1] ESV.

My pencil was blunt, dull, and needed sharpening. My wife had the sharpener, so I asked. "Can I borrow the pencil sharpener?" A few moments later my pencil, no longer blunt, was sharpened and ready for purpose.

There are times when we can pick the dull pencil up and begin to scrawl away over the page. Only to see that the lines - words are thick dull, smudged and sometimes quite blurry. Simply because we had not bothered to take the time to sharpen the pencils lead before starting. Taking those precious few moments of preparation before we begin helps to make the words and the lines stand out crisp, clear and well defined, on our sheet of paper, not smudged or blurred, but sharp and easy to read.

As we come to spend some personal time with the Lord and write our daily journal with Him, don't just rush straight into the process, but take a few moments of preparation time in His company to sharpen your own spiritual lead. Bring what you are about to do before the Lord and acknowledge Him as your guide, allowing Him to sharpen your perspective, hone your mind, to bring things clear crisp and defined by Him clearly to your mind.

Don't just pick up your notebook and start scrawling away with that blunt blurry pencil outlook of your own, but take the time to actually allow God's clear perspective that comes through the Holy Spirit to take precedence in your thoughts. Engage with the Lord and receive input - guidance - direction and fruit to form and take place in your thoughts before writing them down and committing pencil to paper.

Allow His words of life, light and encouragement to flow through your sharpened pencil, your spirit. Don't just fill your page with your own dull flat dead lifeless words that actually say and mean nothing and miss out on what God is trying to say to you with His power-filled words of Life that could, quite possibly, change your very future.

Start your day by inviting Him to sharpen your pencil and your outlook with a thank you, Lord.

The Gateways

1. Zaccheus was a rich tax collector who desired to see Jesus for himself, and who went to great lengths to do this as seen in Luke 19 v 1-10. The result of his actions led him to encounter the Truth and his life, his viewpoint was changed, not only his but also his whole household. Invite the Holy Spirit to Sharpen your perspective as you read this scripture and journal that which He reveals to you. Zaccheus went to great lengths to see Jesus and hear what He had to say, are you prepared to put yourself out to hear what God has to say to you?

2. Can you think of others who allowed God to Change their perspectives? Gideon, Judges 6, Joseph, Matthew 1 v 18-25 are two examples to set you off. Will you allow the Holy Spirit to change your perspective or will you remain dull, blunt and have a smudged blurry outlook on the things of God?

3. My Wife loaned me the pencil sharpener, sometimes we need the help of someone else, someone that we trust, to pray with us, to help sharpen our perspectives and to help us to see things more clearly. If you are struggling to get focus and see then ask someone you trust to pray with you.

14

RECOGNISING FALSE DIRECTIONS.

Let the peace of God rule in your hearts.
Colossians 3 v15[1] KJV.

Over time the footpath sign has become disfigured or moved and is no longer pointing in the right direction. The helpful voices, that have gathered around you, give multiple choices of which way to get to your destination or how best to deal with the problem you have at hand. All of these voices that are swirling around have in fact caused conflict, doubt and uncertainty to enter into your thoughts. Which one, if any, is actually telling the truth and pointing me in the right direction?

How do we know which is the right choice to make, the right direction to take, or the right response to make to someone? Job was surrounded by three so-called advisors, that had gathered around to comfort and assist him, questionably, in his grief. At the end of the book of Job, God calls him to pray for these three and tells him that He will deal with them Job 42 v 7-11. Three advisors who had fed Job with their wisdom and ideas, not the words of God, were not helping Job to move forward in his time of need.

Satan is often referred to as the accuser of the brethren, the deceiver, and a liar. He desires to keep you in the dark, in confusion and he will feed you with all kinds of false directions. He will heap condemnation, self-recrimination, and all manner of negativity onto you, so as, to keep you lost and confused, just stumbling around in the dark. Whereas God is love, He is light, He is someone who is all out for your good and He will feed you with the truth. God will build you up and He will guide you along the path of Life. How do we know if the signpost I am looking at is right and pointing me in the right direction, does it match up with your map {His Word}, your destination {His plan and purpose} or with your inner satnav {The Holy Spirit}? Does it agree with and confirm that which God has already said to you? Satan's question to Eve in the Garden was, "Did God say," putting her into that place of confusion and leading her in the wrong way causing her to question and doubt, the truth - the words of God, in her mind.

What about what has been said is it accusatory, fear instilling, does it put you into doubt and confusion, darkness? If so then it's not coming from the God of Peace, that's the enemy's tactics leading you astray, or does it give you a sense of peace? How does God guide, through peace Colossians 3 v 15 says "Let the peace of God rule in your heart", the word rule here, means Umpire. Let the "peace of God be your Umpire" as to what's right and what's wrong. Remember God is good and He is not a liar. When He directs you it will be in line with His word, with what He has already said to you, and with the plan and purpose that He has given you. It will leave an aroma of heaven in your nose. It will give light upon the darkness and confusion that is facing you and it will give you a way forward. God is an encourager one who will build you up and strengthen you in the right way. He will encourage you to take the right direction, this is the way not left not right this is the way, the way of life, walk in it. Isaiah 30 v 21 Proverbs 4 v 25-27

If He is drawing you away from something in your life that is not of him then you can be sure the enemy will want you to stay with it. If God is directing you down a certain route you can be sure it is good for you and will be of benefit to both you and to others around you, it will be a way of life and not death.

The Gateways

1. Jesus tells us that His sheep know His voice. John 10 v 4 . You may not think you know His voice but Jesus himself said we do. Read about Elijah hearing and recognising God's voice in 1 Kings 19 v 9-13. Can you relate to this? Take time out with God and wait patiently for the clamour and pressures of life to clear and allow the still small voice to speak into your life. Write down what God is saying to you and what he is leading you in.

2. The Holy Spirit will recall all things to our remembrance John 14 v 26. What things will He recall to your remembrance? Spend some time in His presence asking Him to recall things to you.

3. Psalm 37 v 23. Psalm 40 v 2. Proverbs 16 v 9. Proverbs 3 v 5-6[NLT] Jeremiah 10 v 23[NIV] Read over these verses and journal what they have to say to you, personally.

15

EXPLORING YOUR THOUGHTS?

We destroy arguments and every lofty opinion raised against the knowledge of God, and take every thought captive to obey Christ.
2 Corinthians 10 v 5[1] ESV.

Is this a good or bad practice? The Bible clearly tells us to take every thought captive, 2 Corinthians 10 v 5. So which thoughts do we need to take captive? All of them, take every thought and not just those which are contrary to or against the truth of who or what God is and has said. We then are told to lead these thoughts to the obedience of Christ. We take them captive with the truth, did God say or am I being tempted to make a wrong decision?

To entertain wrong thoughts or to explore them more deeply, is to give them credence, to give them life and roots, allowing them to grow and develop. To think upon wrong thoughts will only make way for more to come, for that initial thought to bear fruit and produce more bad thoughts. Have you ever allowed your thoughts to run away with themselves, or allowed a thought to grow and develop just to see where you might end up with it? David did precisely that whilst looking out of his window, he explored his thoughts and allowed them to grow into lust for another's wife, Bathsheba.

John the Baptist preached "Prepare ye the way of The Lord[2]." In other words, you prepare the way or turn your eyes upon Jesus who is the way the truth and the life. Your eyes are gateways, so what we see - think upon or expose ourselves to comes through what we look upon, dwell upon or give attention to. So turn your eyes from looking at and your mind from thinking about wrong things. That which you think upon will develop, it will produce vivid pictures within your mind that you can see quite clearly as you play them out in your thoughts. During a particularly stressful time that I was going through this was in fact, something I used to do on a daily basis, I would explore my thoughts, and my what-ifs. It was certainly not a good or a healthy practice to participate in. I would take a single thought and then in my mind start having a conversation with myself about that thought, painting a picture of problems and troubles that simply grew out of that first thought. This just led me deeper into more and more anxious stressful wrong thoughts which in their turn would lead me into a darker and darker picture. The cycle would not stop until I took action and literally had to rip myself away from that which I was thinking upon. I had to forcibly turn the tape off that was playing havoc with my thoughts and put my mind back onto the good things of God. As John said, "Prepare ye the way of the Lord." In the process of doing this I was in fact turning my eyes towards Jesus, repenting and handing over the initial problem to Christ. 2 Corinthians 10v 4-5[3]. "For the weapons of our warfare are not of the flesh but have divine power to destroy strongholds. We destroy arguments and every lofty opinion raised against the knowledge of God, and take every thought captive to obey Christ." It was not an easy process but a battle and one that I had to keep repeating until eventually, it ceased to trouble me. If I find these thoughts trying to creep back in, I will shut them off far quicker now.

So turn your eyes, prepare the way, to see the truth, life, and good things. Every good gift and every perfect gift comes down from the father of lights, James 1 v 17[4] ESV. Good thoughts are from above, 1 Timothy 4 v 15[5], tells us to meditate to think upon good things. This meditate is think upon, and when God the Holy Spirit reveals something to you, think upon it, take time to explore these thoughts in the company of The Holy Spirit and see in your mind's eye what He is wanting to reveal to your heart. As we think upon good or bad we are exposing our hearts to these things. Exposure to the bad allows fears, doubts and misgivings to enter in. Exposure to good, God's thoughts, feeds and nourishes us allowing life to rise up within and produce a healthy crop of joy, peace, confidence and expectation, helping us to grow in the gift of life given by the father of lights. Reject the father of lies, darkness, and bad thoughts and think upon that which is good, pure, true, honest, just and lovely, Philippians 4 v 8.

The Gateways

1. The word captive in 2 Corinthians 10 v 5 means to bring under control. Obedience here means to submit, so we bring those thoughts under control as they submit to the authority of Christ. Read how Jesus brought His own thoughts captive as He prayed in the Garden of Gethsemane. Mark 14 v 32-42. How might you bring things to The Lord?

2. Satan tried to tempt Jesus away from His calling. How did Jesus deal with the enemy's words and temptations that He heard? Matthew 4 v 1-11.

3. If I want to explore a wilderness area I have never been to before, I might take a map, a compass and a guidebook to that area. What would you take with you to explore your thoughts with God?

16

STORMS.

Meanwhile, the disciples were in trouble far away from land, for a strong wind had risen, and they were fighting heavy waves
Matthew. 14 v 24[1] NLT.

Storms of life can be difficult places in which to keep your feet, to remain upright, as the circumstances of life can so easily sweep you away. The Bible frequently encourages us to stand firm. Winter storms tend to come rolling in, one after another, beating against our doors. In Matthew 14 v 22 - 33 ESV, the disciples, at Jesus' direction, are in a boat rowing against a storm that is beating against them with force. The different Bible translations use words such as, constrained, made, insisted or compelled. Jesus didn't just direct the disciples or ask them to get into the boat, he made them. Why did he do this? Possibly because they were seasoned fishermen, they didn't have the latest Radio Galilee weather forecasts, they knew from experience how to read the signs, how to interpret the sky, they were tuned into weather watching, their very lives depended upon it. They probably knew that a storm was brewing, you can just imagine one of them saying, "I can feel it in my bones". Matthew 14 v 24[2] says, "But the boat by this time was a long way from the land, beaten by the waves, for the wind was against them". The word wind here means, violent agitation, tempestuous force, these seasoned fishermen were where they were at the Lord's command, right in the midst of this great violent storm. Sometimes we can feel as if we are in the midst of a great storm of life and that it is overwhelming us as if we are sinking and all is lost. Yet in verse 25 it goes on to say Jesus came to them walking on the sea. The very Sea that was doing its utmost to sink the disciples and their boat. The very storm which the Lord had sent them out into.

Whatever the opposition is that you're facing, whatever the storm that has been thrown against you, Jesus will never leave you or forsake you He is right with you. Joshua 1 v 5[3], says "I will not leave you nor forsake you." This cry of

God is as true today as it was then [it is repeated in Hebrews 13 v 5[4],] for He himself has said I will never leave you nor forsake you.

Jesus comes walking over the top of whatever the storm is that's beating against you Matthew 14 v26. In John 16 v 33[5] ESV, Jesus warns us and then encourages us, "In the world, you will have tribulation. But take heart, I have overcome the world," He had put it under His feet. The word tribulation is interpreted in different translations as, trials, troubles and sufferings. When the disciples saw him they cried out, not out of recognition but of fear, in the midst of a fear-enshrouded mind the Lord Jesus personally identifies himself to them in Matthew 14v27 . Take courage be of good cheer, it is I it's me I am here stop being afraid.

There are 3 things for us to look at here.

Firstly. Take courage/ be of good cheer, change your countenance change your outlook.

Secondly. Move your focus from the storm to focus on Jesus, from your problems to the solution to the way forward to Jesus.

Lastly. Lift Jesus up in the midst of it and welcome Him into the middle of your waterlogged boat with praise and thanksgiving, 1 Thessalonians 5 v 16-18. Psalm 34 v 1, stop being afraid.

How do I do this, eyes on Him? He who led you into this in the first place, it is He who is your deliverer He is the way. Right in the midst of the storm in the presence of the Lord, there is always room, time, for a miracle to take place Matthew 14v29. Peter at the Lord's command and direction walks on the water. In the midst of the storm that is breaking against your door and with our eyes on the Lord we get to walk all over the top of that storm putting it beneath our feet and to see a miracle of God's deliverance hard at work in our lives. Jesus entered into the boat and immediately they were at the shore. He delivers us safe through the Storms. When He tells you to be somewhere doing something and you are, but finding it impossible to do, know that He is The God of impossibilities made possible and that He is also your Deliverer.

The Gateways

1. Are you at this moment in an awkward position, one that you believe The Lord has compelled you to be in, watch for Him, Call out to Him and know that what He has called you to he will complete. Thank God for His faithfulness

2. The Lord had given them a destination, Matthew 14 v 22, and sent them on their way, then The Lord turns up and delivers them to that destination. In the midst of your storm are you expecting the Lord to deliver you safe to your destination or not? If not then we need to know that the Lord is true to His Word. Ask the Holy Spirit to help you see that the Lord is faithful to His Word. Ask Him to help you see that His Word does not come back empty but full. Thank the Lord that He is in the boat with you.

3. How do you live out your day-to-day, expecting the next great storm to hit and the hatches are already battened down tight, or in the expectancy of the Son to shine brightly?

17

BUILDING AN ALTAR.

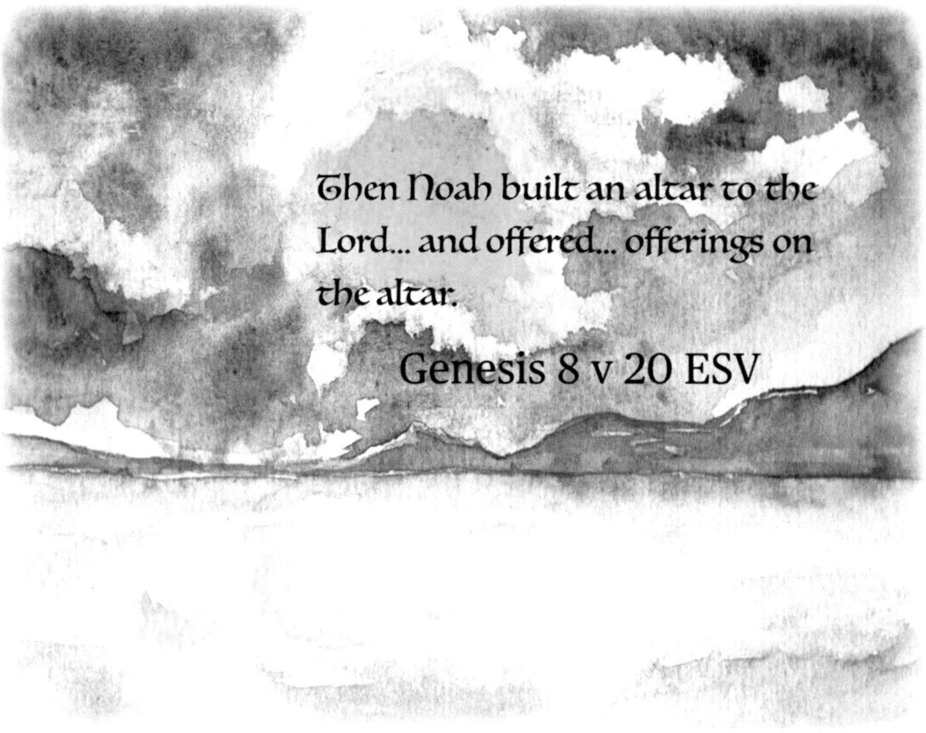

Then Noah built an altar to the Lord…
and offered… offerings on the altar
Genesis 8 v 20[1] ESV.

Throughout the old testament, people would build altars, an encounter with the Lord often resulted in that person building an altar to the Lord and sacrificing on it something that was pleasing and acceptable to Him. Elsewhere we read how some folks would build altars to false gods and sacrifice. Whichever it was it involved building and then sacrificing.

Jesus himself was the ultimate sacrifice, a life laid down so that we might live and live life more abundantly John 10 v 10. Altars that people built after an encounter with God were altars of thanks and remembrance, giving thanks for what The Lord had just done and remembering what had taken place, all that He had just delivered them from or through.

Noah in Genesis 8, after having been shut-in for over a year, steps out of the Ark and onto dry land. He and his family had just been delivered through the storm, the mighty flood and had arrived safe, just as God had promised them. Noah is now standing on dry land and the first thing he does is to build an altar and give thanks, an offering of praise. Genesis 8v21[2] in the Amplified Bible goes on to say that it is a pleasing odour a scent of satisfaction to His heart. This is something to see and take hold of - "Giving thanks pleases God's heart," shouldn't that alone encourage us to be more thankful.

Building altars also takes place to false gods, what is a false god? Anything that we set up against the truth, that we deem to be more important and takes our eyes off God. We are warned not to forget what God has done and God himself says beware lest you forget and elsewhere it says do not forget. Once we start to have a relationship with "Did God say" we start to build an altar of doubt and lies. Those lies begin to steal your joy, which is your strength, your peace which allows darkness, confusion and doubt to enter your heart and mind.

Building an altar of thanksgiving and remembrance is lifting up the goodness of your Father God. It's fixing, etching and engraving into your heart all His blessings, the good, from the very smallest of things and making way for more and greater to come, we give thanks. Jesus gave thanks for the small boy's lunch which made way for the larger blessing of being able to feed the multitude that was sat before him.

Be careful you don't build altars to fear, to lack, to shortage, altars of how can I manage, how will I live, how can I do this. Instead, build up your altar of thanks to the Lord our God. Remembering the good that he has done, the promises that he has made and the truth that he has revealed to you. Build up that Altar of gratefulness to the God of Abundance, to the God from whom all blessings flow. Build thanks, remembrance and gratefulness into your daily day, as you do this, that altar of fear, doubt and confusion will be dismantled and your altar of thanks is risen up, producing a pleasing and acceptable aroma in your heart and Gods. Light always overcomes and disperses the dark.

The Gateways

1. The Lord commanded Joshua to carry up 12 stones from the Jordan once they had crossed so as to remember how God had delivered them Joshua 4.

Spend some time with the Lord and draw up stones of remembrance from times when God has done something wonderful for you. Write them down as you recall them building up your Altar of Thanksgiving as you go.

Remember we overcome the enemy with the blood of the Lamb and the Word of our Testimony, Revelation 12 v 11[3].

2. Put together the stones you have just gathered and form them into a prayer of thanks to the Lord, knowing as you do you are overcoming the works of the enemy. 2 Corinthians 10 v 4-5

3..If you are struggling to find something to give thanks for, then start building your altar with Praise for who God is and what He means to you, as you do this write down the things that the Holy Spirit will recall to your remembrance of the goodness of God in your life.

18

ANCHORS.

Hebrews 6/19.ESV.

We have this as a sure and steadfast anchor of the soul, a hope…..

We have this as a sure and steadfast anchor of the soul, a hope that enters into the inner place behind the curtain Hebrews 6 v 19[1]. We have a steadfast anchor of the soul and that steadfast anchor is hope. The Amplified Bible puts it this way, "This hope [this confident assurance] we have as an anchor of the soul [it cannot slip and it cannot break down under whatever pressure bears upon it]—a safe and steadfast hope that enters within the veil [of the heavenly temple, that most Holy Place in which the very presence of God dwells][2]." The Greek word here for the soul is psyche[3] which refers to the seat of our emotions, feelings, our very being, our Soul, our Heart.

This hope that goes all the way, from our innermost being, our heart reaches right to our heavenly Father and back again. A hope that gives your feet something, although physically unseen, yet rock-solid for you to stand upon.

To remain in position we need anchors. Ships are held in position by their anchors. Buildings have ground anchors. We also need an anchor to keep our position. Jesus is the rock, but what is holding you firm, what is keeping you in position. How do I maintain this position? Jeremiah 31 v 17[4] says "There is hope for the future declares the Lord." Our future has hope. Hope that is spoken by the mouth of God, the very mouth that created everything, Genesis 1 & 2. God himself creates our hope. He is The Creator.

Jeremiah 29 v 11[5], "For I know the plans I have for you declares the Lord plans for welfare and not for evil to give you a future and a hope." God knows your future. God knows the plans he has for you, he put them there. His plans for you do not include evil, that's the enemy. But plans for your welfare, that's your welfare, we fare well, prosper, grow, do good in him, God's plans include hope.

What does our future involve, hope? A hope that He knows that He gives us. The hope that He instils in our hearts and minds is a steadfast hope that is rooted, born and fixed in Him. It is not a false hope a mirage, a shadow, but an anchor, it is something that holds us firm on the rock. A Hope was sown into our very being by our Father God which grows and gives place to faith, that is a certain knowledge, our hope becomes solid. That hope is born out of love, love of a father, love of a son for a father and a father for his son. A hope that is based on a love that would die for us that would go through the cross for you and for me. Not for all of us collectively but for each one of us individually. He didn't die for a job lot of humankind, he died for me personally and he died for you personally that we might live and that we might live more abundantly. My hope is in a God that holds me close, holds me dear, holds me in His hands and delivers me whole, a God that has my best intentions at heart. He is a Father God that will cause me to fare well whatever the storm of life that I might find myself in.

The Gateways

1. There are times and instances when the life that we know all around us can come crashing down and it is quite a scary frightening time. Rahab the prostitute went through such a time as the city in which she and her family lived, came crashing down, Joshua 6. Her house had actually been built into the city wall of Jericho, Joshua 2v15. As the city walls came crashing down all around, Rahab's home, in which her family was sheltering, remained standing and did not come crashing down. She had anchored herself by hoping in God, the symbol of that hope, a scarlet cord, the

blood of Jesus. Read in Joshua how Rahab the prostitute and her family became grafted into God's family. Who or what is your safety anchor in times of trouble?

2. Noah's Anchor to God delivered him and his family through the flood. The challenge for Noah wasn't just the building of the Ark and the verbal abuse he received, but also the drifting on the water cooped up in that boat for over a year. What do you think Noah and his family did to keep themselves in the right place with God and what might we be able to do as we wait for the Lord to deliver us?

3. As you face difficult, challenging, times what comfort and encouragement can you draw upon by reading these two stories and others? How might you implement some of these things in your own life?

19

GATEWAYS.

I am the way, and the truth, and the Life. No one comes to the Father except through me. John 14 v 6[1] ESV.

Gateways are an important part of our lives. They are something that we have to pass through in order to go from one place to another, from the street to someone's garden we pass through a gate. Towns can often be named the gateway to a certain country or area. Passes through mountain chains are referred to as the gateway to the land or region that lies beyond. The first Homesteader Pioneering families of the American West had to find gateways/passes that gave them access through the Rocky Mountains and onto the Pacific coast. To enter into ancient walled cities you had to pass through a series of gateways. These are all examples of access points that move you from one place to another.

The most important gateway we can ever pass through is our Lord Jesus Christ. Through Him, we gain access to the heavenly kingdom, to the very presence of our father God and eternal life.

Jesus said no one comes to the Father except through me. There is no other way to gain access to our Father God except through the Gateway, the Open Door that is our Lord Jesus Christ.

We are told that the way to enter His gates is with thanksgiving Psalm 100 v 4. Thanks are then followed by praise.

Ten lepers were healed. One of them, a Samaritan, returned to Jesus to give him thanks, as a result, he was not just healed but made whole [Sozo. Be - make whole] Luke 17 v 19.

Revelation 3 v 8 tells us that He has set before us an open door that no man can open or shut. An open door/gateway means an open opportunity an invitation and if that open doorway has been set before us then God sets open opportunities before us. How do we enter in, through that open door, this opportunity that has been set before us, we enter His gates with thanksgiving in our hearts? So surely we must enter into all that God sets before us with thanks. This thanks is not just lip service but it is an attitude of your heart, a thankful heart. Through the gateway of a thankful heart, the Samaritan leper moved from a place of healing to a position of wholeness.

King David was always thanking and praising God and we often hear about the keys of David. Thanks and praise bring us into the fullness and very presence of God himself our father. To walk forward through an open doorway a divine gateway an open opportunity we do so not by ourselves but in union and unity with the son Jesus who leads us into all that the Holy Spirit is revealing to us. The fullness of the promise of God. We walk forwards with thanks and praise, live this day that the Lord has set before you with a thankful heart and a song of praise on your lips. You may be amazed at where it moves you into.

The Gateways

1. In 1 Corinthians 16 v 9 Paul refers to the opposition he received after a door of opportunity was set before him. Should we expect an easy walk into what God has set before us or should we be prepared for opposition?

2. David was a practitioner of thanksgiving, how do you approach something that God is setting before you? With a thankful heart and expectation or an attitude of it's mine, I deserve this, I've earned it, I worked hard for that.

3. Read and pray over Luke 17 v 11-19, the Leper that returned to God to give thanks, 10 Lepers walked through the Gate of Healing, one returned to give thanks. In thanksgiving what did this one leper receive that, apparently, the other nine did not? What other Gateways do you think God might set before you?

20

A PLAN AND A PURPOSE.

Who knows whether you have not come to the Kingdom for such a time as this. Esther 4 v 14[1] ESV.

God has a plan and a purpose for each and every one of us. This plan is woven within us, it is part of our very being, the fabric of who we are, and it is placed within us from the beginning of time. We have been birthed into this world not by chance but for just such a time as this Esther 4 v 14. God knew us before we were ever born. Jeremiah 1 v 5, Ephesians 1 v 4.

This plan and purpose are divinely connected to the Father. "I know the plans I have for you, declares the Lord." Jeremiah 29 v 11[2], that's plural, not singular. God has more than one thing for you to do. I know the plans I have for you, God's plans not man's plans. When men got together with men and devised a plan to build a tower God intervened, it was not Godly, it was not a good thing. Man can also hear God's plans and then try to do them his way, not God's way as with Joshua and the fortress of Ai, Joshua 7 & 8. They were going the right way taking possession of the land, but without God's guidance or direction and they were going about it in their own way, they had forgotten to look to God, to include Him to put Him first. People died and Joshua was defeated.

John was in the river baptising people just as he had been called to do. Jesus, the Son of God comes along to be baptised but John tries to prevent him, Matthew 3 v 14, he tries to get Jesus to do it his preferred way however Jesus explains to him how it needed to be done. John received correction on the matter, is obedient to the plan and purpose for his life and baptises Jesus, God Himself, John a man baptises God, how awesome and wonderful is that.

The bible tells us that man makes his plans but God directs His steps, John had his plan laid out, Jesus baptises me then I baptise Jesus, but God directed his steps. The bible also tells us that we will hear a voice guiding us, not that way don't go right don't go left this is the way these are the steps walk in them, Isaiah 30 v 21.

David had the complete plans for the building of the temple from the porch right through, room by room and even how to decorate it 1 Chronicles 28. Did he put his own plans together did he just make it up. No. All he had written down David had received by the spirit, 1 Chronicles 28 v 12[3]. David the king was obedient to God, he didn't build the temple, that would be his son Solomon's purpose. He didn't take the God-given plans which he had in his possession, and try to implement them himself, no, he was obedient to what God had said to him.

When you sit down to make your three-year, five-year, short-term - long term plans for your life make sure that first of all, you seek God about your life and like David write down all that he says to you. David had to pass it on to Solomon. Habakkuk 2 v 2[4] ESV, tells us to write the vision down clearly so that whoever reads it may run with it. Solomon ran with what David had written down and built a most wonderful temple.

God gave me a plan and purpose, a long time ago now, I wrote it down and left one small bit out that I wasn't keen on and then asked some trusted friends to pray over what I had written down, one of them came back to me with the exact piece I had tried to leave out. Go with God's plan, listen and write down all that He says even the parts you are not so keen on doing.

The Gateways

1. Joshua did not consult God, he did as the spies said, "Do not have all the people go up, but let about two or three thousand men go up and attack Ai. Do not make the whole people toil up there, for they [the enemy} are few."... Joshua 7v3[5]. Once Joshua gets back in line with God we see God's direction in 8 v 1[6], And the Lord said to Joshua, "Do not fear and do not be dismayed. Take all the fighting men with you, and arise, go up to Ai. See, I have given into your hand the king of Ai, and his people, his city, and his land". How do you approach your work, what's laid out in front of you, by asking God for guidance or do you rely on your own strengths and abilities? Why do you think it is important to include God in your day-to-day job, workplace or daily schedule?

2. Why is it important to spend time listening to God?

3. Why is it important to write down/journal what He has said to you?

21

EVERYTHING UNDER CONTROL.

Luke 22 v 42[1] ESV.

Not my will, but yours, be done.

Isn't that how we like life to be, under control? I know what I am doing and I know when I am going to be doing it. One thing is for certain though, there will always be uncertainties in life. Yet how often do we try to take a hold of those uncertainties and plan around them, making sure that no matter what it may be that comes our way, the outcome of it is, that we are always in control of the situation with the solution right at our fingertips?

We, however, as Christians, are clearly called to lay our lives, wills and yes even our plans, down and to become living sacrifices for Christ, trusting in God for all that we need.

Even Jesus himself only did what he saw and heard the Father do. In the garden of Gethsemane Jesus asked his Father for things to change, not just once but three times he asked, for what he knew was coming next to alter, and then He laid His own will down on the altar of sacrifice and said "Not my will be done but yours Father," turning all control of his life over to God. As we walk along in our lives, a life which incidentally was given to us by God our creator and our Father, there is a fine line between holding onto control of our life in our own way or a life that has been laid down for God's purposes.

The disciples' lives were forever changed when they laid down their lives and let go of that control of what they were doing, fishermen busy mending their nets ready for the next day's work, to fishers of men. To hear the call of Jesus and then get up and walk away from controlling what they did to following Him, Jesus, wholeheartedly.

Matthew walked away from his tax collector's job, a very lucrative, powerful position, to follow the call of Jesus, Luke 5 v 27-28. He did just that, he got up from his tax collectors booth and walked away from it, just like that.

When we do actually remove both hands from the steering wheel of our lives and look to Jesus the author and finisher or perfecter of our faith, we move from our own worldly controlled day-to-day and into the area of a life laid down. We move into the realms of living by the divine guidance of the Father, Son and Holy Spirit, leading, guiding and directing us along the way in which we will see the Glory of God revealed in our lives.

Which job should I take, what is my vocation, what about my husband/ my wife-to-be, Lord show me the way. When we look to our Lord for all that we need and acknowledge that He is our provider. We let go and by doing so we are acknowledging that Jesus is the Lord of our lives. We open up our hands, unclenching our fist-like grip with which we have been holding tight to everything. Hands which are raised up open in praise and thanksgiving are hands that are open and ready to receive. In just the same way a mind that is open to divine guidance is receptive, but a mind fixed on I've got everything under control is closed. Lay down your life, open your eyes, ears and heart to all that God desires to give to you.

The Gateways

1. We read about Matthew the tax collector giving up his booth to follow Jesus. What do you think it means to give up everything and follow Christ? Write down your thoughts on this.

2. Read in Matthew 19 v 21-22 where Jesus asked a wealthy young man to do something first and then Come Follow Me. The young man couldn't bring himself to do it. Why do think this was so?

3. What would you find the hardest thing to lay down and why? Then ask Jesus for help in laying it down at His feet and acknowledging that He is Lord of your life.

22

TAKING A SNAPSHOT.

Son of man, look with your eyes and hear with your ears and set your heart upon all that I shall show you.
Ezekiel 40 v 4[1] ESV.

Photographs are pictures of memories, snapshots of things we have seen and done, they are images of times gone by. Snapshot by snapshot we can build up a photo album, a collection of moments captured as a pictorial reference, that we can return to and look through whenever we choose to.

We have the ability to do exactly the same process within our minds, building up a pictorial reference catalogue, snapshot moments of different events that we have come across and focused on, only this time not with your camera lens but with your eye. The more we think about a particular something, whether we have seen it or heard it and focus upon it, the more we will develop that particular something within the dark room of our mind. Be it good things or bad we determine what pictures we allow to enter into our minds and become imprinted for us to develop and focus upon at a later date, to recall, remember and then to go on and further develop them. Have you ever noticed that with just one single photograph that has been taken in the past, which you now have a hold of and are looking at, we can then with the aid of our dark room developing gear, imagination combined with our memories, we can add to it, recalling a whole host of other events that may or may not have happened around it? Likewise, when we focus on something it has a way of developing and growing within our minds if we allow it to.

The same thing happens when we listen to the deceptions of the enemy and focus upon them picturing them and what may, possibly, be the eventual outcome, the what if's. That deception will grow, develop and become an album itself full of bad snapshots, false pictures, misconceptions and lies.

God always encouraged his people to remember the good that he had done and to pass it on to others. He encouraged Joshua to draw stones of remembrance out of the river Jordan so that they would remember the good, Joshua 4 v 1-24.

Jesus as he sat with the disciples at the Last Supper,1 Corinthians 11 v 24[2] said to them "Take eat, this is my body." He was calling them and us today to remember him, to picture him. We can build up an album of his goodness to us within our minds.

In Philippians 4 v 8[3], we are encouraged to think upon that which is true, honourable, just, pure, lovely, true, noble, admirable, excellent and praiseworthy. Think upon such things.

Our Father above is the Father of good gifts, good things, James 1 v 17. He is not the Father of bad gifts.

We are encouraged repeatedly, throughout the Bible to give thanks, why, because as we do so, we are not only picturing in our minds good things but focusing our minds on the goodness of our God, and entering His gates, Psalm 100 v 4.

The enemy has come to steal to kill and to destroy, don't focus on the bad images he is flashing past your eyes or whispering in your ear he is after all a joy stealer. But I Jesus have come that you may live and live life more abundantly John 10 v 10.

As we go through our day taking mental snapshots of the good things, we start to put together our pictorial albums of God's goodness. As we do this moment by moment, day by day, we will find that those good pictures will grow, multiply, and bear a harvest within our lives of good fruits. Such as well-being, joy, goodness, happiness and healing which in turn will lead to producing more snapshots and more albums of the good things that God gives us. Fix your eyes on lies and very soon your days will become a very dark unhealthy environment and within that darkness, it can become quite hard to see something good. God's promises are rainbow-coloured and his garden is full of beautiful flowers that will fill your mind's eye with good pictures if you look for them.

The Gateways

1. Part of the joy of having a Photo album is looking through it with others. How can we do this with the good things of God and who might you share these memories with? Ask the Lord to lead you as to who to share these moments with. What God gives us is meant to overflow to others, family, friends, wherever or whoever He points you to. Someone who is sitting in darkness may need to hear the goodness of God that you have to share.

2. As you read through Philippians 4 v 8 and the list of things to think upon, how does this compare to what is generally running through your mind? Are there certain areas, thought patterns, that you need to change? What about any old photo albums that you have stored up within your mind that need throwing out? Ask the Holy Spirit to help you identify these areas and deal with them. Why not take your camera or your mobile phone and make a point of going out and taking some new photographs of the beauty around you? Thank God for a new photo album of His Goodness to you.

3. One of the most important things to remember is to make space for The Lord in your life, in order that we can make some new good memories with Him. Do you make space for Him? Ask Him to fill your thoughts with Him. Ask the Lord to help you refocus.

23

DEVOTED TO DESTRUCTION.

Let love be genuine. Abhor what is evil, hold fast to what is good. Romans 12 v 9[1] ESV.

Throughout the book of Deuteronomy we read over and over again the Lords direction for His people to cross over, enter into, and possess the land that He is giving them. As we move into the book of Joshua we see in chapter 1 v 11[2] ESV where Joshua is relaying the Lords command to the people and saying, "Pass through the midst of the camp and command the people, 'Prepare your provisions, for within three days you are to pass over this Jordan to go in to take possession of the land that the Lord your God is giving you to possess." The word possess in Hebrew is yaras[3], which means, to possess, to occupy by driving out the previous tenants and occupying in their place. Put it another way, here you are this is yours I'm giving it to you, if you want to own it you're going to have to drive out all the opposition, devote it to destruction.

Joshua then comes face to face with, The commander of the Lord's army, who tells Joshua in chapter 6v5[4], "And when they make a long blast with the ram's horn, when you hear the sound of the trumpet, then all the people shall shout with a great shout, and the wall of the city will fall down flat, and the people shall go up, everyone straight before him." When the walls of Jericho come down, go straight up and take possession of the city that I have given you. Joshua had seen first-hand what happens when you don't deal with the opposition. He had been here before, 40yrs ago, when apart from himself and Caleb everyone else of his generation had turned away from what God had promised them and questioned what he had said, allowing the opposition to remain.

The people are being charged to go, straight up, straight in, no hesitation, no deviation, no turning left or right, no trying to make allowances, changes of mind or heart. Straight up straight in. Evict the enemy. Later on, in Joshua 10 v 39[5] it talks of, "Being devoted to destruction." This is your land possess it, drive out and destroy the enemy. All trace is destroyed even the city itself has been raised to the ground, nothing left. The enemy stronghold completely destroyed.

Today we may not be driving people out of their land but we are dealing in just the same way with the works of the enemy, thoughts and to be more precise wrong thoughts.

Romans 12 v 9[6] in the ESV tells us to abhor what is evil. Which means utterly detest it. The NIV says hate what is evil, love what is good. The prophet Amos simply says Hate evil Love good.

2 Corinthians 10 v 5[7] "We destroy arguments and every lofty opinion raised against the knowledge of God and take every thought captive to obey Christ". The word captive means to bring under control, to subjugate or to conquer.

Thoughts can come knocking at our door, speaking to our minds and whispering in our ears. Whatever it is needs dealing with if it's something that God is saying to you then it requires your full attention. If it is some unwanted salesman, the enemy, trying to sell you something you don't want then we have to slam that door shut and not let him get his foot over the threshold, don't give him even the slightest toe hold into your life. The works of the enemy are to be abhorred, detested, have no time for them. If it is coming against that which you know to be true Romans 12 v 9 then it needs to be destroyed, devote those thoughts those niggling doubts to destruction.

Trample them down underfoot with that which you know to be true. What did God say? Know your God, 2 Corinthians 10 v 5. Remove those walls of opposition with obedience to what He has said to you. Don't give the salesman and his lies any substance by listening to them. Devote those lies to destruction. Whilst you are devoting these things to destruction it's interesting to note that the word Devote also means, to consecrate, consecrate by giving it to God. So by removing the enemy's lies and devoting them to destruction till no trace of them is left, I am also taking ground that the Lord has given to me, consecrating it. This is the truth, this is holy ground, this is the promised land and I am putting it under my feet. I am standing upon that which I know to be true. Just as the Commander of the Lord's Army said to Joshua in Joshua 6 You are standing on Holy Ground. The next thing Joshua had to do was utterly destroy the opposition, Jericho.

The Gateways

1. The Promised Land was already occupied, Joshua was commanded to destroy those occupants and take possession. How might we apply this to our daily walk with God? How do you come against the lies that may be occupying your thoughts? What is it that is stopping you from moving forward into all that the Lord is giving you? Ask the Holy Spirit for clarity and journal all that He has to say to you.

2. Have you noticed that when God wants your attention a whole host of alternatives can come flooding in. How might you deal with this sort of occurrence, do you give the alternatives your attention or do you sweep them out of the way?

3. I have heard it said that in order to spot a forgery you need to study the original. How can studying God help us to destroy lies or fakes?

24

IT'S IN THE DETAIL.

The shepherds returned, Glorifying and praising God for all the things they had heard and seen, which were just as they had been told.

Luke 2 v 20[1] NIV.

Have you noticed how God is a God of detail? Joshua 15 v 1-12 describes the boundaries of the land allotted to the tribes as their inheritance. There is nothing vague about what is theirs and where they are to live, He has given a precise outline, boundaries, for them to live within.

When it comes to building something God is just the same, never changing, precise in the detail. Just read in Genesis 6 v 14-22 the description of something that has never before been seen or come across in the world. The Ark, a boat in which to carry animals both big and small, was given to Noah and would also house within it his family and deliver them all safely through the flood that was about to come. Noah was a farmer, not a boat builder, but the plans he was given by God were precise even down to which wood to use and how to make it watertight.

We can also see the description of the tabernacle given to Moses, Exodus 25-26, how it was to be erected, laid out and furnished. Precise in detail.

Solomon's temple, the plans of which were given through the spirit to King David, Solomon's father, to give to his son. Detailed. 1 Chronicles 28.

How to find a certain baby laid in a manger, Shepherds sat on a hillside out under a starlit sky, heard the directions and went and found him just as they had been told Luke 2 v 8-20. The wise men read the prophecies about a saviour king, they didn't just sit under the heavenly stars but read them and followed what was being said in them, following what was revealed in the detail which also led them to that same baby boy, Jesus, our saviour Matthew 2 v 1-12.

These are just a few instances that show us a God who is so involved in the detail yet so connected to revealing what's hidden. In the New Testament Jesus, our Lord, opened up their minds so that they might understand Luke 24 v 45 and in the Old Testament, we read how Ezra, the scribe, taught the people that they might receive the sense Nehemiah 8 v 5-8. Today we have been given the Holy Spirit, our teacher, who recalls all things to our remembrance John 14 v 26.

So what about me today, feeling lost, who am I, what am I supposed to be doing, how am I supposed to deal with this situation, this problem. God your God has the answer to all your questions and he is just as involved in the intricacies and details of your life as he was for all those we have mentioned above. He is after all your father, your creator. He is the author and finisher of your faith. He is the reason we are here today, he is your guide and your light. He is your life and what's more for those of us who are Born Again, He dwells within us John 14 -15-16. Open up your heart to him and allow him to reveal the boundaries, the purpose, the life that He has called you to live and not just to live but to live this life more abundantly.

The Gateways

1. Recall a time that God gave you directions on something He wanted you to do. How did that guidance affect you, did you choose to follow it or did you dismiss it and what was the outcome?

2. Boundaries can often be looked upon as restrictive. Can you think of areas where boundaries not only help you but actually bring you freedom and enable you to do something that you otherwise could not have done?

3. Why do you think it might be important to know your boundaries?

25

A NUT OF HOPE, A LIGHT IN THE DARKNESS.

Why, my soul, are you downcast? Why so disturbed within me? Put your hope in God, for I will yet praise him, my Saviour and my God.

Psalm 42 v 5[1] NIV.

A nut, a kernel, or a seed is something through which new life can spring from or it is something that, when inwardly digested, can provide us with much-needed sustenance.

Someone very close to me was struggling with lies that the enemy had been feeding them for some time, lies that they were struggling to cast off. One dark night whilst dealing with fears and anxieties of my own regarding that person's health, I watched as they personally picked a nut to eat, chew on bite into and inwardly digest. That simple act of selecting and eating a nut filled me with such hope, a shaft of light was breaking through into my own darkness giving me hope for the future. That act was, for me, a direct answer to prayer, it was something that caused me to break down into tears after what had been a very difficult day. That difficult day was in fact the culmination of a string of previous difficult days that lead up to this one moment, this nut of hope.

But even in the darkest of times never forget God is good and always to be praised, that God never forsakes us or leaves us. God always listens to our prayers and answers.

When we draw closer to Him he draws nearer to us. So the nut, what about it, as that nut was selected and chewed I immediately felt God prompting in that a seed of hope had just been sown. A nut, a kernel, is a seed and a seed sown will produce a crop. A seed of hope will give fruit to faith. This led me to rise up in my own faith, a faith which the enemy had been besieging with his lies. But this seed of hope, this nut, was fortifying my own faith that in turn strengthens the feeble knees - the tottering knees - the limp arms. A seed of hope was planted for that future crop. Seeds are for the future for another day. A nut of hope, God's word is that kernel that contains the truth that once chewed on and inwardly digested will produce a crop that will strengthen our bodies and our minds, that will feed us nourish us and enlighten us.

When you are looking out for the bigger miracle, watch out and listen for the still small voice that is speaking hope into your ear. For the small thing that is taking place right in front of your eyes, right before you. Don't be blind to the works of God. When someone or something takes hold of a nut of hope, a seed, give thanks to your father, give thanks for the small things that make way for the greater crop that is to come.

The Gateways

1. Have you ever walked along a dark path at night without a torch fumbling your way through the darkness and then in the distance seen the welcoming light of your destination? How did it feel to see that light in the distance? How hard was it to follow the path in the dark?

2. When you're trying to navigate your way through a personal storm, how important is it to have hope? How can you see hope in the midst of a storm?

3. Can you recall a time in your own experience when hope has helped you through? Take time to praise God and thank him for that seed of hope sown into your life.

26

ADMITTING THAT YOU'RE WRONG.

This is the way, walk in it.

Isaiah 30 v 21 ESV

This is the way walk in it.

Isaiah 30 v 21[1] ESV.

There has only ever been one perfect person and that was Jesus Christ, the Son of God, born into this world as a child. Walking about amongst us until his death upon a cross. The rest of us are not perfect and we all make mistakes, we all get things wrong. Jesus said "Father, forgive them, for they know not what they do" Luke 23 v 34[2]. The problem comes when we do actually know that we are in the wrong and refuse to admit it and change our ways. This is where we step into the realms of pride, Proverbs 16 v 18[3], says "Pride goes before destruction, and a haughty spirit before a fall". We also move into the realms of an unteachable spirit, a hard heart, "I know best. I don't need any help". This way of acting, thinking or behaving will then put us in a position of opposition to God, who is our helper, for He is always helping and encouraging us to walk forward, to see the error of our ways and to change them. Isaiah 30 v 21[4] "And your ears shall hear a word behind you, saying, "This is the way, walk in it," when you turn to the right or when you turn to the left". We are in fact choosing to ignore and do our own thing.

Zacchaeus a wealthy chief tax collector had a life-changing encounter with Jesus. Having lived his life in a certain way until Jesus confronted him with the truth and instead of arguing and sticking to his old ways he changed giving back to those he had wronged and as a fruit of this, salvation came, not just to him but to his whole household and changed the very atmosphere within his home. Luke 19 v 1-10

Peter had a vision of a blanket lowered down from heaven in front of him that was filled with all kinds of creatures Acts 10. Along with this vision came the command arise eat. Peter replied no, no unclean thing can pass my lips. The heavenly reply to Peter was, Acts 10 v 15[5] "Do not call something unclean if God has made it clean." Three times this vision and command were repeated before Peter finally got the picture and arose in agreement his heart and mind changed. To have remained in opposition would have been an act of stubborn, prideful, "I know best" arrogance which would have been the same as that of the Pharisees whom Jesus referred to as stiff-necked. Peter's admittance to the fact that his old way of living, in the light of the cross, was now wrong opened the way for the first gentile believers to be received into the Kingdom of God and filled with the holy spirit.

Admitting where you are wrong and apologising, saying sorry or repenting of that wrong way of thinking, of living, can open the way not just for right living with the Lord but for the entire atmosphere in which you live to change, alter and allow the very air that you breathe to freshen and for the staleness that you have been living in to go. Stubborn refusal to change gives off a bad air, a bad smell, not a sweet aroma. That change of attitude may even open up the doorway for a mighty work of God to come pouring through, for a miracle to take place. Don't be so shuttered up to change that you shut out the light of what God is wanting to reveal through you in your life. Be open to correction, be open to the work of The Teacher, The Holy Spirit as you move through your day.

The Gateways

1. How do you respond to the knowledge that you're wrong. When [A] someone else points it out to you. When [B] God points it out to you. When [C] you read something through which you see that you have been wrong. Write down your response to these and prayerfully consider your answers.

2. Zacchaeus made a spectacle of himself by climbing up a tree to get a better view of Jesus. Can you think of a time you stepped outside of your box, so to speak, to get closer to Jesus?

3. Has there been a time in your life when you have really held on to some point or position, knowing it was wrong? How did that make you and those around you feel, such as your family or your household or your friends? When you finally let go how did things change? If you are still knowingly holding on to something you know to be wrong then I urge you to ask The Lord to help you let go.

27

THE RIVER OF LIFE.

Then he said to me, this river flows east through the desert into the valley of the dead sea. The waters of this stream will make the salty waters of the dead sea fresh and pure.

Ezekiel 47 v 8[1] NLT.

The prophet Ezekiel in Ezekiel 47 describes how the river flows out from the throne room of the temple through the land and down to the sea. Describing how by increments this river gets deeper and deeper until, finally in verse 5, we cannot possibly touch the bottom but are swept up in it.

Verse 6 calls the prophet back to the river bank so that he can see what actually lies beyond that point of full immersion. Standing on the brink of the river he is called to see and things he had not previously been able to see are revealed and pointed out to him. There are trees whose roots draw nourishment from the river, their leaves are for healing and for food. There are places from which we can cast out our nets and receive provision. Then there is also the point at which the river enters into the sea - the dead sea. As the river enters into the salty seawater, it cleanses, refreshes and purifies the water. It goes on to say wherever the river goes is life, everywhere the river goes lives.

Revelations 22 v 1[2] also tells us that the river of life "sparkling like crystal". The very name of the river, *The River of Life,* shows God's intention for us as his people, to have life. Everywhere that river goes lives, this river carries within it life, healing, refreshment, purification, food, provision for your work, and places for you to cast out your nets and receive. All that is needed for life is contained within the River. The ESV says as it[The River] enters in things become fresh. Before Ezekiel can get to see or understand any of this the first thing that he has to do is to respond to the call of God, Ezekiel 47 v 6[3]. "Son of Man have you seen" and then he is led.

When places in your life become stale, unpalatable or lifeless they need freshening up and purifying, the dead sea is full of salt and nothing can live there. The good news here is that the river of life brings freshness as it enters in. So listen for God's prompting as he calls you to see, look for the area of your life that God is wanting to cleanse, freshen up and reinvigorate. Let the river of life enter into these areas and cause your life to sparkle and flow, Revelations 22. How is your health, your marriage, your friendships, your work, your outlook, family, church life, is it sparkling and flowing? Then allow God's river of Life to enter in. Giving access for the river to flow freely into these areas is going to bring new life, fresh life, and a sparkling life that flows directly from the throne of God through you.

If we choose to be, stale, stubborn, lifeless then we become one of those stagnant salty pools where the river doesn't enter in. It doesn't enter because we refuse to respond to that call from God, Son of man see. Listen to His call, lay down your life and allow that river to enter fully into your day this morning bringing fresh new sparkling life of God with it. Allow his river of life to fully wash over you and for you to become fully immersed in him, fully.

The Gateways

1. Spend some time with the Lord asking Him to show you the areas of your life that need refreshing.

2. The trees for healing and the trees that feed draw their nourishment from the river of life. Are there areas of your life, both physical and spiritual, that need nourishing and healing? Allow God to Feed you with His Word and for His Word to heal and nourish you in your mind, body, and heart[soul]. Psalm 107v20

3. As you walk forward today, recognise that God is our provider, not you and that He alone provides for all of our needs. Thank him for the river of life and that he has provided a place for you to cast your nets.

28

THE ONLY TRUE GOD.

I am who I am.
Exodus 3 v 14[1] ESV.

Have you heard there is only one true God and it's not you? It can be a hard pill to swallow and one that ultimately Pharaoh couldn't. I am that I am came knocking at his door through a man named Moses, called by God. God said to Moses, "I AM WHO I AM." And he said, "Say this to the people of Israel: 'I AM has sent me to you.' Exodus 3 v 14. God describes himself throughout the Bible as the only true living God and that there is no other. Throughout the old testament, we hear thus saith the Lord. It is important for us to know above all else, even our own opinions, that God is God and that there is no other, Isaiah 45 v 5. He is the Father of all Creation and we, His children, need to know both what He is saying and that He, God, is actually saying it. Bible scriptures can so easily be misquoted, taken as gospel from what someone else has said, and we don't even take the time to read it for ourselves we just adopt it as the truth. We can even take a rigid stand on a particular scripture only to find out later that it's not even in the Bible. Did God say?

Others have erected their own images of a god and worshipped them. God refers to it as doing evil. In 1 Kings 18 v 19, we see how the prophet Elijah stood against the combined force of 450 prophets of Baal and 400 prophets of Asherah and challenged them to a duel. All of you verses my God for whom I stand. As the 450 prophets called upon Baal, a false god to act, nothing at all happened. We can even see how Elijah mocks them in 1 Kings 18 v 27[2], And at noon Elijah mocked them, saying, "Cry aloud, for he is a god. Either he is musing, or he is relieving himself, or he is on a journey, or perhaps he is asleep and must be awakened." Then it's Elijah's turn, he calls upon The One True Living God and the fire of heaven is unleashed, burning up all that which had been set before Him. Elijah, one man, then goes on to destroy those 800 plus prophets of Baal, 850 to 1, overwhelming odds? Not for God.

When we stand in God's name be sure you're following his directions, operating on his guidance. Don't allow pride to enter in, don't allow your ego to take centre stage, "I'm doing this for God." Don't forget what he said to Moses I am that I am is sending you, don't send yourself and then expect God to back it. God sent Moses to Pharaoh to do and carry out his directions, and his words. In doing this and through his obedience many signs and wonders came to pass and the whole of the Hebrew nation walked away from slavery, released from over 400 years of bondage, just as God had said in Genesis 15 v 13-16. Moses was a conduit through which God the great I am was working and making His presence known. There are times when we can get beyond ourselves and it becomes us who are trying to release the people from bondage for God, instead of which we are actually erecting and lifting up an image of self. All of a sudden we elevate ourselves our opinions and thoughts above God, this makes us a false idol. God will not suffer that and before long there will be a fall, an outcry an outpouring of our own will in action, perhaps through frustration, annoyance possibly, overflowing into anger or rage that someone or something is not responding or happening quite as we would expect it to. This is a good point at which to see that you've overstepped beyond the mark and to repent, laying your life, your will, your take on an issue, down and acknowledging that God is God, He is the great I am and allowing him, the Holy Spirit to flow through you. After all, this is not about you but Him, His glory to be revealed, through you, to the life of the person that is standing before you, that God is ministering to through you. It's not your problem to solve but God's and what's more, He already has the answer. God may use you to speak into someone else's circumstances or situation that is causing a problem. God will give the solution to the problem, allow him to speak through you. Cast all your cares and your burdens at his feet, He lives in and through us, He is the great I am not you. When we speak we should speak his words which he gives us not our own. Allow God to flow through you a river of life bringing life and freedom that has the power to set captives free.

The Gateways

1. When you have stepped out for God, who do you think should get the acknowledgement, you or the Lord and how does it make you feel?

2. When you see an answer to someone's problems come about, how do you respond, Oh I've done well there? Or do you respond to what has happened by praising God and giving Him thanks?

3. When God asks you to do something do you respond positively to His request of you, question why, or do a Jonah, disagree with what God is doing and walk away in the opposite direction?

29

HEALING.

Every good gift and every perfect gift is from above, coming down from the father of lights, with whom there is no variation or shadow due to change.

James 1 v 17[1] ESV.

Did God make me ill? No. "Every good gift and every perfect gift is from above, coming down from the Father of lights," James 1 v 17[2]. Your heavenly father is a giver of good gifts, sickness is not a good gift. He does however work all things to the good for those who love him Romans 8 v 28[3]. Jesus, God's son, is a man yet God, he died on a cross and took all sickness upon himself that we his children might live abundantly. God's will for us is to be healthy, to grow, to flourish and to abound in this life. We can see this in Jesus' ministry as He went about healing people of all their diseases. However Satan the enemy comes to steal your health, your joy, your peace, to kill your hope, and to destroy, he is not a goody he is evil and to be abhorred, all his works are to be detested, hated. Not lived with, not suffered, but crushed in whichever form he tries to come into your life with. Sickness is one such thing.

God heals in more than one way. Ezekiel 47 tells us that the tree's leaves are for healing. Medicine through the ages has discovered it to be true. Herbal remedies have been used throughout history and still are today for the treatment of countless ailments. We are discovering more and more hidden cures within all sorts of plants throughout the world. Luke of the gospels was himself a doctor, a physician.

Luke 10 v 30 - 37. A man was robbed and left in a ditch for dead. He needed help and he needed aid, yet even the church the representative of God walked past on the other side and left him. A Samaritan stopped and gave assistance to this person, tending to his needs and taking personal care of this man. God brings healing through others that come into our lives solely for that purpose. He will bring someone to help, aid and assist you in your recovery.

Luke 7 v 11 - 17. Jesus reached out to a widow who was about to bury her dead son, he reached out in compassion as the funeral procession crossed his path. Raising her son from the dead and restoring him fully alive and fully well to his mother, there's no record of her crying out for His help. He is a loving, compassionate, God who simply heals.

Acts 28 v 3 - 5. Paul, the Apostle, was bitten by a poisonous snake, he shrugs it off into the fire and the locals expected him to die, Paul however expected to live. The word of God to him was that he must go to Rome, Paul knew his destination he knew God's word to him and he shrugged off the serpent into the fire, he was healthy whole and well.

Many times throughout the gospels we can read record after record of how Jesus healed everyone, that came to him, of all of their diseases.

Luke 8 v 43 - 48. A woman who according to traditions, to the law, should not have been anywhere near Jesus, pushed her way through a crowd and then she reached out and touched him. She had had an issue of blood for 12 years and was considered unclean and could possibly have been stoned for her actions. In her need she reached out to someone she had heard heals, she reached out and touched Jesus. Far from reprimanding her, Jesus calls her to Him, commends her faith and pronounces her whole.

James tells us that if any amongst us are sick we should go to the Elders and be anointed with oil and prayed for. James 5 v 14.

There are many more accounts of how God heals, through his people, see Elijah, Elisha, the Acts of the Apostles and then on down through the ages, countless records of God healing.

We can take scripture and speak it out over ourselves. Sometimes seeing an instant result and other times taking time for his word to bear fruit. God heals. Oh, but what about if I have unbelief.

Mark 9 v 17 - 27. A Father stands desperate with his son, who has terrible fits, before Jesus. The disciples were unable to help and this father is asking, [As a father myself, I can picture him standing there, before Jesus, with tears in his eyes], he is literally crying out to Jesus for his help. Jesus calls him to just believe and the father responds "I believe; help my unbelief."[4] Jesus' response, "Can't help you, you will have to come back when you believe." No of course it wasn't. He is a God of love, of compassion, and cares for us. He knows your heart, knows your thoughts, and provides for all your needs. This father was crying out for help and Jesus, despite the father's lack of belief, healed his son by casting out a demon. The Amplified Bible, Mark 9 v 24, say this. "Immediately the father of the boy cried out [with a desperate, piercing cry], saying, " I do believe; help [me overcome] my unbelief."[5]

Whatever position you may find yourself in know this, God loves you and desires for you to be well, to be whole, to be healed, and set free. Whether you consider yourself to be unworthy, unclean, or unbelieving, God heals. The word of God itself says He is our healer and that he sent his word and healed us of all our sicknesses.

Isaiah 60 v 1[6] says Arise, get up out of the depression the circumstances that have held you and shine (live, glow, sparkle with health) Amplified Bible.

As a personal note, I have seen God heal on multiple occasions, in my own life, my family's lives and others God has directed me to, not one of these times was a replica of a previous time, each healing has been different, yet each one was to the Glory of God. Some healings have been instantaneous whilst others have taken a period of time. There are some healings that we are busy thanking God for and waiting for.

The Gateways

1. Why should I be bothered to find out what the Bible says about healing, I'm well, there's nothing wrong with me. Read Luke 10 v 30-37 and be prepared so that you don't walk past someone in need of prayerful help because you don't know what to pray or how to respond.

2. Do you believe God heals today? If not, then ask God to help you to see the power of His healing love that has touched countless lives in many ways.

3. Is healing only about physical needs? What other areas in our lives, do you think can be healed? For example, broken relationships, Mental Health, Self Esteem. Are there areas in your own life in need of God's healing touch? If so, then spend time with the Lord and talk to him about whatever it may be that ails you. Thank Him for healing, after all, it does say, By his wounds you have been healed. 1 Peter 2 v 24[7].

30

DESIRING TO DO GOOD.

Therefore choose life.
Deuteronomy 30 v 19 ESV.

There are times in life when you may encounter something, some situation that can cause you to find it hard to believe that God's heart is towards us and not against us. That God is desiring to do good towards us. To believe that He is not the one desiring to harm us, but actually, to do us good. In Deuteronomy 30 v 15 - 20, Moses is passing on to the people the things that God has said to him, concerning life and good or death and evil. In these verses we see the Lord urging His people to choose life and good. He is desiring good for us. In Deuteronomy 30 v 19[1] the Lord says "That I have set before you life and death, blessing and curse. Therefore choose life, that you and your offspring may live."

It's our choice to make, we can choose good or bad - life or death. God, desiring good for us, advises which choice we should make, *choose life* He says *that you and your offspring may live.*

The Father God also sends us His son Jesus Christ, who came that we might have life and live this life more abundantly. That's the father's desire for us to "LIVE" and live our lives more abundantly through him. Jesus said of himself "I am the Way the Truth and the Life. No one comes to the Father except through me." John 14 v 6[2]. God is even pointing out to us, through his son Jesus, how we are to come to Him, He is desiring to have a relationship with us. He himself is Love, is good, is joy and He is showing us, telling us how to gain access to all His goodness that He wants to share with us. It comes through His Son Jesus. It's our choice Life or death.

He desires for us to live our lives in a land full of promise, a land of milk and honey, his land of inheritance that is set out before us for us to possess and dwell in Joshua 1. It is a fruitful land, his desire for us is to be fruitful.

His desire for us in Isaiah 60 is to shine[3], which means being surrounded and resplendent with light.

His desire for us is to receive good gifts that he the Father of Lights gives us. James 1 v 17

His desire is for the lonely to live amongst family, he is after all a family man. Psalm 68 v 6

His desire is for the sick to be healed and those possessed set free, Jesus' command to the disciples as he sent them out Matthew 10 v 8. As Christians, we are followers and disciples of Jesus Christ.

His desire is to see people building one another up, encouraging one another, Paul's words in 1 Thessalonians 5 v 11.

His desire is to walk with us in a garden, His garden planted with us in mind Genesis 2-3.

His desire is for a man and a woman to be united in love, Genesis 3, it is not good that man should live alone. That unity, togetherness, is love. He, God, is love and his desire is for us to live together in him with him and to walk with him.

His desire is to have a fruitful relationship. Him with us, us with Him. His son is the vine and we are the branches but He, the Father, is the vinedresser causing us through his care and husbandry to bear much fruit John 15.

His desire as Jesus said is for us to do all the works that he did, his miracles, and to actually even do more John 14 v 12, wow how good and amazing is that.

Know this, God is for you and not against you, God loves you unconditionally. Jesus His son died on a cross for you that you may live. God's desire for you, choose life, choose to follow Jesus this day, for He is the way the truth and the life.

The Gateways

1. Why is it important and what do you think it means to choose to follow Jesus on a daily basis.
2. Does following Christ exempt me from troubles. Read John 16 v 33.
3. If I am going through troubles how can I believe that God desires good for me. Read Romans 8 v 28.

31

A PROPHECY OR A PROMISE? SPOKEN AND GIVEN.

Deep in your hearts, you know that every promise of the Lord your God has come true. Not a single one has failed. Joshua 23 v 14[1] NLT.

From the very beginning of the Bible, God speaks and it happens. In the creation record on the very first pages of Genesis, we see that God speaks and it is so, let there be light and there is light. No if's no but's, it happens just as he had said.

After the fall of man through Adam and Eve in Genesis, there is a shift, a change, now we see or hear how God speaks through his prophets. Thus saith the Lord. What we see here is that God is still speaking, it's still the Word of God that's going forth only now it is through man, the outcome of which is no different, it is so, it happens just as was said. God sends Elijah to King Ahab to say there will be no more rain, instead, there will be a drought in the land and that's exactly what happened for the next 3 years or so, drought, not a drop of rain fell. Then God sends Elijah back to Ahab to say now it will rain and it does, a huge downpour of such magnitude that Ahab has to get home quick or he will be stuck in a quagmire of mud, fruit of all the rain that is now falling upon the land. These accounts can be found in 1 Kings 17 - 18[2].

God speaks through His Prophet, Isaiah Isaiah 7 v 14 in the Old Testament, promising the arrival of a saviour born of a virgin, impossible you might say. But then through the obedience and faith of a young virgin woman, Mary, Jesus the Son of God is born, Emmanuel our saviour. Luke 1 v 26-38

Jesus the son of God then speaks declaring his Father's promises and prophecies out loud and they happen. Jesus himself foretells the coming of the Holy Spirit, a teacher, John 16 v 7, and it is so. The Holy Spirit comes upon man in the upper room of Acts 2 just as Jesus had said. He also through the cross returns to the Father's side seated at the right hand of God interceding for us.

The bible records how God's word goes forth and does not return void but accomplishes that which it has set forth to do Isaiah 55 v 11. It also says that it is, "A resounding yes and amen" to all the promises of God 2 Corinthians 1 v 20[3]. They are not false or empty, they have their fullness in Jesus Christ and will come to pass completely. Joshua tells the Hebrew folks in Joshua 23 v 14[4] *"And you know in your hearts and souls, all of you, that not one word has failed of all the good things that the Lord your God promised concerning you. All have come to pass for you; not one of them failed."*

Paul has been told by the Lord that he must go to Rome, Acts 23 v 11[5] The following night the Lord stood by him and said, *"Take courage, for as you have testified to the facts about me in Jerusalem, so you must testify also in Rome."* This word is then spoken to Paul again onboard a ship in the midst of a terrible storm, Acts 27 v 23 - 26[6].

For this very night there stood before me an angel of the God to whom I belong and whom I worship, and he said, 'Do not be afraid, Paul; you must stand before Caesar. And behold, God has granted you all those who sail with you.' So take heart, men, for I have faith in God that it will be exactly as I have been told. But we must run aground on some island."

He has been told the same thing again by the angel of the Lord, you must go to Rome. Paul is delivered safely through the storm despite the loss of the ship torn to pieces by the submerged rocks of a hidden reef, he is also protected from the bite of a poisonous snake, Acts 28 v 5 and arrives in Rome to speak about the Lord, just as God had said he would.

What has God promised you, what prophecies have been spoken over you, what words of God have been placed into your heart and mind to speak out loud? Declare them on His behalf over yourself for as you speak these words, they are going forth, released into this earthly realm to accomplish all that He wills to be done. These words, prophecies, and promises that you hear and receive are busy at work moulding and shaping you ready to do that which He has intended ordained anointed and called you to do. If God has said it then you can be sure it is true and it will come to pass.

The Gateways

1. It is a good practice to journal words of God, promises, and prophecies that have been given to you and then to go over them and water them with thanks. God keeps His Word. Deuteronomy 11 v 18 is a description of how the Hebrew people kept God's promises in front of their eyes. How do you keep God's promises fresh in your heart and mind?

2. Paul on the ship during the storm said, until all hope of being delivered alive was gone, in this position he was encouraged by an Angel of the Lord. Are you struggling in a storm as you wait for the fulfilment of a promise of God to come to pass? Thank God for encouragement, thank God that He sustains us and delivers us. Think back to other times in your life when God's promises have come to pass for you and give thanks for those times for the goodness of God.

3. Go over the Word that has been given to you and ask God for confirmation, for encouragement as you wait on Him.

32

ARISE EAT AND DRINK.

1 Kings 19 v 7[1] ESV.

"Arise and eat for the journey is too great for you."

After pouring himself out doing the Lord's work and dealing with the prophets of Baal, Elijah finds himself at Beersheba[2], which means, Well of the sevenfold oath. Elijah then distanced himself a days journey from the well of oath, or the promises of God.

Elijah was sitting and sleeping under a Juniper tree, which is actually, Genista or the Broom tree or shrub. This shrub has yellow flowers and a bitter root, Elijah was sleeping on that bitter root, he was low, tired and feeling sorry for himself, depressed. 1 Kings 19 v 4[3], And he asked that he might die, saying, "It is enough; now, O Lord, take away my life, for I am no better than my fathers." Then the Angel of the Lord steps into the picture and gives Elijah instructions on how to strengthen himself.

1 Kings 19 v 5-8[4]

And he lay down and slept under a broom tree. And behold, an angel touched him and said to him, "Arise and eat." And he looked, and behold, there was at his head a cake baked on hot stones and a jar of water. And he ate and drank and lay down again.

And the angel of the Lord came again a second time and touched him and said, "Arise and eat, for the journey is too great for you." And he arose and ate and drank, and went in the strength of that food forty days and forty nights to Horeb, the mount of God.

Elijah is being fed and watered with what he needs to strengthen, nourish and sustain him by an Angel of God, divine provision for his needs. In order for it to do him any good, he had to rise up, take hold of it and eat it.

Without food and drink we cease to be, we cannot live without them. Psalm 23 v 5[5] says our Father has set before us a table. This is not a little side table or a refreshment stand, this is a king's table, so-called because the meaning of which - sulhan[6] - according to Strongs H7979 is -- a table [as spread out] by implication, a meal - table. It is a table that is extended and spread out before us, it isn't just a king's table either but this is the King of kings table, this is the Lord's table that he has set before us. This is God's table decorated and prepared specifically for us, with our name on it. Laden by him for us to feast upon, dine on, eat from. This is the table of Jehovah our provider. What do you need, come to the table and eat, it's here exactly what you need to nourish your body, soul, and spirit. Eat, feast, drink, what's on the menu is especially for you.

Jesus gave his disciples bread and said this is my body broken for you, eat. This is my blood poured out for you, drink. We eat, we drink, we live. Elijah was told to "Arise," which means, to get up, to rise, to abide, to continue. In order for Jesus to rise up, He, first of all, laid his life down. For us to arise we must first be laid down. My life, my will, my flesh, laid down, my cares, worries, hopes and desires, all laid down. Then he stands by your side and says "Arise," get up, live, eat and drink. The father has laid out what he wants you to eat he has placed it before your eyes, now feast upon it, devour it, abide in it and drink it in. The word drink can also mean imbibe like a drunkard. We soak, drink in the Spirit of God, soaked and saturated in the Holy Spirit. Drink of his blood so freely poured out, receive the Spirit of God, receive refreshment. God's table is there to nourish us and refresh us. Are you hungry, are you thirsty for the things of God, come to me, come to my table, and dine on that which I have prepared for you?

We need to eat and drink, it gives us strength. Strength to continue, strength to go on. Without it, we grow tired weary and faint. Eat and drink do not become fearful. The table is prepared in the presence of your enemies, up-close presence, not distant looking on but up close staring over your shoulder. Eat of my body drink of my blood, strengthen yourselves in me, look to me, eat and drink, arise eat and drink. And Elijah did so in 1 Kings 19, he arose ate and drank not once but twice, eat and drink and continue to do so it's the only way to live. Eating and drinking are a daily requisite.

The Gateways

1. What do you think it means, or refers to, for us to arise eat? Elijah was called to Arise eat. How does this relate to you in your daily walk with the Lord?

2. How important is it to feed upon God's Word and how often do you think we should do this? We are encouraged to fix our minds upon Him, how does this relate to feeding on God's Word?

3. Which do you think is the most important? Reading as much of God's Word as you can in the time you have or to meditate on a portion of Scripture that catches your attention. As a new Christian **!!** years ago I thought if I read the Bible through from start to finish, then I needn't bother to read it again as the Holy Spirit would just be able to recall it to my remembrance afterwards. Guess who didn't get away with that one? My Wife used to really encourage me to read it,[to strengthen and encourage myself] she even gave me her own bible and would pray that I would read it. Thank you Jesus for a Godly wife and an answer to her prayers. I now love reading my Bible and the most exciting part is getting to read it with the Holy Spirit and allowing Him to stop you in mid-sentence so that He can teach you something new. Don't rush and get indigestion but take time to digest what He is feeding you. Ask the Lord to give you a renewed refreshed desire to read His Good Book. Possibly just as Elijah did and just as I did, you may find that you need someone that will come and stand alongside you and encourage you in your walk with the Lord.

33

LIVING IN THE HOUSE OF GOD.

And man became a living soul.
Genesis 2 v 7 KJV.

If I was asked to picture a house it would probably have four walls, a roof, windows and a door. However there is another meaning of the word, house, and that is family. So living in the "House" of God can and does mean living in and being part of His family. Not just as a visitor who has just popped in, for a look-see, as we sometimes are when we go to have a look inside some ancient house of God such as a Church building or Cathedral. We can stand amazed in these places,[I certainly do] at the awe-inspiring craftsmanship that has gone into the making of some of these incredible buildings from times long ago.

We are in fact a far more incredible piece of craftsmanship, our bodies having been created, sewn together, and crafted into shape by the Master Craftsman Himself. Our Father God, by His very own hands in the garden of Eden, moulded out of the very earth itself and then having His very breath, His life breathed right into us. Genesis 2 v 7[1]. *the LORD God formed man of the dust of the ground, and breathed into his nostrils the breath of life; and man became a living soul.*

The human body and all of its intricate complexities that are used daily, every moment of every day and night, is mind-bogglingly amazing. For instance, the way in which your hand and eye just co-ordinate together thousands of times a day in a multitude of different ways and tasks, just think about writing a simple sentence on a page. Or how your body identifies what is good to eat and what is bad, by taste, smell, sight or all three of these senses combined. To the actual process of breaking down your food, inwardly extracting all that your body needs and discarding what is not. Simply amazing and beyond my own understanding. This body of ours carries around within it, our brain, our heart and our soul.

Jesus says that he, the son of God, will come and live in us, make his home within us, and also the Father as well as the Holy Spirit. John 14 v 20-26[2]. Living within us, within our hearts and minds and soul. Our Spirit becomes sealed in him, protected, safe and incorruptible. This body crafted by God and brought to life by his very breath becomes a house of God in which He lives. The New Testament refers to us individually as the Church, not the building but the people, themselves and how each individual person connects and joins together to form that Holy Temple in which the Spirit dwells. Ephesians 2 v 19 - 22[3]. Incredibly it goes on to say in John that not only does God the triune Godhead live in us but we live in him. Our life is no longer a single solitary bedsit-styled life but a multi-faceted life where we live in a symbiotic style of life, where everything we need comes from our Father in Heaven through His Son Jesus and all that we do is connected through the Spirit to heaven.

Heaven in a sense does come down to earth as we move around carrying the Father, Son, and Holy Spirit with us. Jesus lived and operated in this way as he walked amongst us on earth, communing constantly with the Father and He said that we could live life in this way with him. A house a family of God, living moving daily in him with him and through him. Arise shine for the Glory of the Lord has risen upon you. Don't forget today that you are a living breathing house of God, a walking living part of the family of God. Rooted, grounded and connected to Him.

The Gateways

1. God dwells within us and we in Him. If he was to physically stand next to you, would you alter any aspects of your life? If so make a list of what needs to go and ask God to help you to change in these areas.

2. Knowing that God is with you, how does this help you in your daily routine? Does this make you view or look at your Life and the things involved in your life differently?

3. What does it mean to you to be part of the House of God, a family member? Is it a new revelation to you? Is it important to you? Or is it something you have never really thought about and just taken for granted?

34

WALKING FORWARDS INTO FREEDOM.

Forgetting what lies behind and straining forward to what lies ahead.
Philippians 3 v 13[1] ESV.

To be able to overcome whatever it is that may be afflicting us, coming against us, opposing us, causing us pain or distress, at this moment in time will involve walking forwards, mentally, physically and of course spiritually forwards. Biblically speaking walking forward equates to some of the following:-

1/ Freedom, the Hebrew people as they walked away from Egypt and slavery. Exodus

2/ Victory, Jehoshaphat and his people as they walked forward against the enemy. 2 Chronicles 20v21[2]

3/ Life, Lazarus as he walked out of the tomb. John 11 v 44[3]

4/ Faith, Peter as he stepped over the side of the boat onto the water. Matthew 14 v 22 - 33[4].

5/ Separation, the Reubenites as they left the other tribes in Joshua and walked forward into their own land separated from the others. Joshua 22

Abram walked forward with the Lord but away from the physical past, he had grown up in. Walking away from the mental connection to that past would take far longer. He had carried Lot and his family with him, responsibility and care that God had not intended for him to take with him, Genesis 12 v 1[5]

Sometimes what is afflicting us now in the present day is firmly rooted in our past and will need unearthing to find the root and to extract it completely. To be able to do this we have the Holy Spirit revealing what it is that needs to change, and what it is that needs to go. The Lord may choose to use others that He sends our way to help us.

Saul had an encounter with the Lord on the road to Damascus on route to deal severely with any Christian followers of Jesus that he could find, Acts 9. Jesus brought Saul's world crashing to the floor, and his pride in who and what he was, a Pharisee of Pharisees, came tumbling down. Blinded he no longer led but had to be led by his men to take shelter in a house, utterly reliant on those around. It took a faithful follower of Jesus, Ananias, to walk forward in his faith, away from fear, possibly mixed with unforgiveness, and go to Saul the Christian persecutors' aid and open his eyes physically and spiritually to the truth. Then Saul had a further time alone with the Lord, Galatians 1 v 11-20[6] where he, no longer a Pharisee, could walk forward into the freedom of what the lord was calling him to do. Even then as he walked forward with the Lord he would be reminded, by those he encountered, of his past and all that he had done.

Walking forward into freedom is a daily walk that we as believers choose to do, clothing ourselves with the presence of God, with His word, His truth, His promises revealed, His will and His love. Casting aside the things that may well be part of our past but are not our present nor our future and they need to be left behind at the feet of our Lord. Just as Paul himself said forgetting what's behind but pressing on. Philippians 3 v 13-14[7]

We change, God, however, doesn't he is constant, He is the same today and tomorrow just as He was yesterday never changing. We, however, do change, we are moulded and shaped by the potter, new life is breathed into us, and we are given a new heart, the heart of God. Our mind is renewed and we become Christ-centred, not self-centred as we walk forwards into the freedom of a life in Christ.

The Gateways

1. Are there areas in your own life that you need to lay down at the Lord's feet and walk away from, just as Paul did?

2. The Reubenites had been fighting to take hold of the promised land for the other tribes. Joshua released them from this and blesses them as they walked forward into the rest of their lives {Joshua 22 v 4-6[8]}. They were walking away from warfare and walking forwards into farming. Is the Lord calling you forwards away from one way of living to another?

3. What would it mean or involve for you to walk forward in, Freedom, Victory, Life, Faith and Separation?

35

THEN HE SHOWED ME.

Fear not, stand still and see the salvation of the Lord, which he will shew to you today.
Exodus 14 v 13[1] KJV.

"Then the angel showed me the river of the water of life, bright as crystal, flowing from the throne of God and of the Lamb." Revelation 22 v 1[2]. This was revealed to the Apostle John so that he would see and know these things of God and then show them to others. It was a personal revelation to John that God fully intended to be shared.

To you, it has been given to know, Matthew 13v11[3]. What a promise, what a privilege, what a blessing that has been given to us, His Children, the knowledge of who our Father is and the invitation to get to know Him deeply and personally, what a gift but it is something that we need to desire, to know Him more. Then he showed me, God shows us and reveals things to us. Are you crying out, are you hungering and thirsting after the things of God, then he's going to show you. Ezekiel, the prophet, was called back to the banks of the river, the river of life, in order that he might see

Ezekiel 47 v 6[4]. John, the Apostle, was lifted up into the very presence of God that he might be shown the things of God Revelation 4 v 1[5]. Jesus, the Son of God, called his disciples up the hill to him that they might receive Mark 3 v 13[6].

We have been called into his very presence, why, to see and to behold his majesty, his Glory, the very things of God. How do we see, by standing still? Stand still and see the salvation of the Lord this day that He will show to you, Exodus 14 v 13[7] KJV. In John 4 v 35[8], Jesus tells his disciples to lift up their eyes to see.

When God is calling you to see something, respond, because he is about to show you something wonderful of himself, something that will bring change [you can't have an encounter with God and remain the same] something that will give life, something that is flowing from him to you.

As we spend time with God reading the Bible, the Holy Spirit will emphasise a portion of scripture, a verse, a word or a few words to you, lifting them out from the text that surrounds it. When this happens don't rush past in an effort to get to the end of your daily read with the intention of coming back to it later. Give your full attention to it there and then, inviting the Holy Spirit your teacher to give you insight, and revelation, into that which the Father is wanting you to see and know. This is one of those moments, just like Ezekiel, where you have been called back to the river, the river of life to behold and to see.

There are hidden depths to the things of God to the mysteries. Jesus said to Peter cast out your nets into the deep for a catch, he did and his net was very full Luke 5 v 4[9]. In Luke 24 v 45[10], Jesus opened their minds so that they might understand, the important thing to see here is that it is God who gives us understanding and not our own intellect. If you want to see to understand then don't rush past or as Peter said Master we have toiled all night and caught nothing, meaning he had been very busy and was tired and weary, don't go past don't ignore the prompt but just as Peter went on to say, at your word Lord I will, and he received an awesome catch. God is a God who gives and gives abundantly and whose desire for us is to delve deeply into His Word, to cast out our nets and receive all that He has to teach us of his ways. His word is a lamp to our feet and a light to our path Psalm 119 v 105[11]. Remain in that position by the river with the word that has been called to your attention and allow the Holy Spirit to open up the net that is your mind and fill your understanding richly and abundantly with what he has for you to feast on. Revelation into that which you have been longing for and desiring. Ask and you shall receive, knock and the door will be opened, seek and you will find. Receive the things of God from God. Behold see.

The Gateways

1. Do you expect to receive teaching, revelation knowledge, from God or not? Whatever your answer ask God to take you deeper into His Ways.

2. Has God ever revealed anything to you personally? How did that revelation affect you at that moment, in your day, or your life's course? Thank God for showing you and ask Him to reveal more of His Truth to you.

3. Life today is very busy and always on the go, why do you think it is so important to Stand Still to see? Jesus also told his disciples to Lift up their eyes to see. What do we need to lift our eyes up from and what do we need to do in order to Stand Still?

36

LEARNING TO LOVE.

You shall love the Lord your God with all your heart, all your soul, and with all your mind.
Matthew 22 v 37 ESV.

God's greatest commandment is to love him with all of your heart, with all of your soul and with all of your mind Matthew 22v37[1]. The next Matthew 22v39[2] is to love your neighbour as yourself. I cannot do either of these, let alone both, without not only God's help but God's love flowing freely through me.

The first says with all your heart, with all your soul and with all your mind. Well, 'My self' is very busy throughout 'My day' focusing on 'Me' and 'My life' - 'MY problems' - 'My cares' - 'My worries' - 'My needs' - 'My tasks' and 'My jobs' that need to be done and then, of course, there is making sure that 'My tick' list is getting full of ticks. How do we get to loving God with all of our hearts, souls, and minds, to begin with, never mind extending that love to those that live around and about me, when I am so busy with all that I have to do in a day?

Learning to love involves learning to trust and learning to let go. God's love is not self-focused, it is not lustful, or self-fulfilling, it's not about getting out of something or someone just what you want or need. A dog will give you a lot more attention when it wants something from you such as a walk or feeding. Likewise, we tend to turn our affections or attention upon someone when we actually want something from them in return. Not so with God, God's love is unconditional. He loves you with all that he is because God is love, it's who he is. For us to love him with all that we are, firstly involves accepting Him into your life, so that He - Love, fills us. This will then open the way for learning. Learning to let go, learning to lay down your life, and learning to surrender, to allow those walls of resistance to come down, to open up and become vulnerable, to let go of control. It is no longer I that lives but Christ who lives in me, Galatians 2 v 20[3]. This verse begins by saying in the NLT, my old self has been crucified with Christ. It is no longer about me. We let go of self, this is no longer 'My life' but the Life of Christ that is living within me. All my cares, dreams, worries and tick lists galore, all of them laid down at his feet. Cast your burdens onto him, lay them all down at the foot of the cross. To surrender, how hard this is, we are taught by this world to survive, to protect ourselves and to fight for what is ours.

Yet the Kingdom of God teaches us to live, life, in a different way, we have to learn to surrender, not my will be done but yours. Jesus said these words whilst on his knees in the Garden of Gethsemane as he poured out his heart to his Father God in heaven. We also need to come to that place and position where we fall to our knees, as Jesus did, and say those words to our heavenly Father. "Not my will Father but yours be done." Surrendering all that we are to God, in the trust that he knows what's good for me and what's more, his way is the best - not mine. Yes, I have plans of my own but as it says in Proverbs 16 v 9[4], "He directs my steps." We need to realise God's plan for us is perfect, whereas our plan is man-made and imperfect. To open up to God means to have a teachable spirit and be willing to be taught, to open up to something new, something different from what we may be thinking or doing, and to be open to the ways and the things of God. We are so used to building walls and protecting our assets to cover ourselves in protection from possibly being hurt. Becoming vulnerable and to actually admit or to say I don't know what the answer is and to actually let go, open your hands and release your grasp, by saying I don't know God but you do, I don't know how to respond, to act, or what to say right here but Lord I trust you to lead me. I don't know what is going on here but I am going to lean on you. The God who loves me unconditionally and cares for me delights in me and reveals his love in me. Love that takes me by the hand and walks me forward out of and away from that worldly love that is driven by my own desires and delivers me into that God-given love that overflows from me into those that are around me. To be able to Love God with all of my Heart needs the miraculous re-creation of God's love in me. Without God in you, you can't love God and love your neighbours selflessly.

The Gateways

1. How do you think or see yourself, lovable or unlovable and how do you think God sees you? If you have answered as unlovable. Spend some time asking God to show you how He loves you, How much He loves you personally.

2. It was several years after I had given my life to Christ before I had a real revelation of His love for me. If you have never experienced the tangible love of God for you then simply ask him to pour out His love upon you. It had me on my knees in tears. Perhaps you need reminding right now of just how much He loves you. This may sound strange to you or even alien, but just ask Him for a hug.

3. We can do things, ministry, church, outreach, talk to our family members or neighbours, all out of a position of duty, expectation, sufferance, or it can come from a place of Love. Sit with the Lord and ask him which position you tend to come from?

37

LEST THEY FAINT ON THE WAY.

I am unwilling to send them away hungry.
Matthew 15 v 32[1] ESV.

Ever felt tired and weary, or that you simply can't carry on any longer, that it is all too much for you?

In Matthew 15 v 32[1] and the feeding of the 4,000 Jesus speaks to his disciples and says "They have been with me now three days and have nothing to eat I am unwilling to send them away hungry, lest they faint on the way." The KJV states he will not send them away. In Matthew 15 v 35, we read that in order to be fed everyone is encouraged to sit at Jesus' feet. Have you ever come to Jesus for feeding, but just been so busy so tied up in what you're doing that you've never actually taken the time to sit at His feet and listen?

Your personal well-being is important to Jesus. The biggest and greatest thing that he did for you was to die on the cross, taking all sin, shame and sickness upon himself that you might live. This selfless act of love is something that we should all know rejoice and give thanks for. There are so many other examples of his love, care and compassion for each of us and Matthew 15 v 32 is one such place. Those who come to him he will not send away hungry, he is not going to let you faint on the way.

Faint on the way, who is the Way and the Truth and the Life, that's Jesus. When we come to the Lord for help the way ahead can sometimes feel a bit blurry a bit feint and not always look clearly marked out as we try to continue onwards, be encouraged to sit at the Lord's feet and receive. Jesus often took time to recharge his batteries by climbing a hill to be with the Father, or out on a boat, or even it says some desolate place. Basically, he took time to be alone with his Father, time for replenishing. if Jesus needed to do this then so do we.

As we walk in the way with the Lord there may be times when we may experience a silence, an emptiness, yet you can be assured that the Lord will not leave you or forsake you. That he is always with us. Isaiah 42 v 3[2] says "A bruised reed he will not break and a faintly burning wick he will not quench". Jesus will not break you or leave you unfed, that is simply not his way as his way is life. He will not leave you in the dark, his way is truth and truth is light which removes darkness.

4,000[3] men plus women and children sat in his presence and every one of them was fed until satisfied not one of them was forgotten or missed out and what's more, there were baskets of food left over. We sit with the Lord and we require feeding on something perhaps healing, provision, family or whatever the issue may be. Sit in his presence and expect to be fed - expect to receive from Him. Sit with the Lord and walk in his way. Remember his heart is for you and it will overflow into your heart and feed you with all that is required until you are satisfied, but know this even when you are satisfied, filled with as much as you can possibly eat, at that moment he still has baskets more left over to feed you with again and again and again, there's always more. We just need to take time, regularly, to sit at His feet and let Him feed us.

The Gateways

1. Ruth sat at Boaz's table and ate all that she could and only then when satiated, full, did she take some home to feed Naomi her mother-in-law Ruth2 v 18[4]. Make sure that when you sit at the Lord's Table, His Presence, that you remain there until you are filled, full, satiated and then you can go and feed those He directs you to. Ask the Lord to fill you with His goodness and then ask for guidance as to whom you could pass on some of what you have gleaned from Him.

2. Discouragement drains and all too quickly we can lose heart. What steps can we take to Guard our Hearts?

3. As the Hebrew people walked through the wilderness God fed them daily. If they didn't gather it in for that day they would go hungry. God feeds us through His word which we daily need to gather in. For the 4000 men plus women plus children to receive their food from Jesus, they had to sit at His feet and receive. Do you sit at His feet? What do you think it means to sit at his feet? Spend some time with the Lord exploring ways in which you might gather in His daily bread.

38

THIS IS MY BELOVED SON.

Listen to him.
Matthew 17 v 5[1] ESV.

Matthew 17 v 5[1] "This is my beloved son" is the second time that the father speaks these words out over his son, Jesus. The first is when John the Baptist, baptises Jesus in the River Jordan. This, the second time, is with Peter, James and John the disciples on top of a mountain, the Mountain of Transfiguration. The difference here is the words, "Listen to Him," as well as the fact that Peter, James, and John had been asked by Jesus to climb up the mountain with Him, in doing so they heard God's declaration over His son.

Jesus is *the Word of God*, he is *the living word*, he is also *The way, the truth, and the life,* and we are called by the Father to "*listen to him.*" To listen to the words of truth, the words of life. The Holy Spirit recalls to our remembrance and points us to Jesus, who is the truth, John 14 v 26[2]. But right now, on top of a high mountain by themselves, in the very presence of God, Jesus is transfigured in front of them. The Greek word for transfigure is metamorphoo[3] which means "To transform, to change into another form". A divine process, of change, is going on right before the eyes of the three disciples.

The Father himself is speaking out those words from a cloud above them, it is not Jesus and it is not the Holy Spirit speaking, but the Father and he says, "Listen to him". Father God is calling and pointing our attention to his son and saying, Listen to Him, Listen to the true and living word, Listen to the Way, Listen to the Light of the World, Listen to the life, Listen to Him. With this Peter, James, and John throw themselves, face first, down onto the ground in fear. They do not do this when Jesus is transfigured white and shining like the sun or when Moses and Elijah appear by Jesus and talk with him, this they seem to take in their stride, Peter even offers to build three shelters for them to stay in. The very presence of the Father, however, puts them on their faces in the dirt, absolutely terrified. Matthew 17 v 7[4] Jesus reaches out to them and touches them saying "Rise and have no fear". When they lift up their eyes they see no one but Jesus, himself, looking down at them. No fear, just the perfect love that casts out all fear 1 John 4 v 18[5], and it is that love that perfect love that transfigures us, changes us inwardly into his likeness. In his presence, there was no fear and all they saw was Jesus, the truth and the life, their friend.

Peter, as he walked on the water, had his eyes on Jesus and in this position, there was no fear, no fear of the waves that were contrary to him, no fear of the unknown of what lay beneath his feet. All Peter could see was love perfect love standing before him, his eyes are fixed on Jesus and Jesus's eyes are looking down on Peter. Peter took his eyes off Jesus and immediately fear entered in and he began to sink into what he was standing on, but Jesus reached out and touched him.

Coming into this place of stepping out into the midst of what is scary and frightening, requires you to allow Jesus to lead you up a mountain a high mountain. Matthew 17 v 1[6], After six days, so on the seventh day, Sabbath day, 7 is perfection. Jesus on the seventh day was transfigured. To overcome some mountains, we need to allow Jesus to lead us up them to climb and overcome them, to place them beneath our feet.

This will lead to a life-changing moment in our walk with Jesus as we overcome with him, casting out and removing whatever that fear may be. As we cast ourselves and it down at His feet and rejoice as perfect love declares over us Rise and have no fear. Just eyes, eyes which are the gateway to your heart, filled with truth, with light, with life, with Jesus. If Jesus is encouraging you to climb a mountain with Him, give thanks, that mountain is about to be placed beneath your feet, as things are about to change. Listen to Jesus calling you.

The Gateways

1. As a Born again Christian we are already a new creation 2 Corinthians 5 v 17[7]. What things do you think may still need to change about yourself? As a child of God do you see yourself as His Beloved?

2. Father God is calling us to Listen to His son Jesus, the Word of God. How can we do this and when should we be listening? Is it important to listen?

3. Are you living in fear of something? Found yourself, terrified, frightened, overburdened. Bring it before the Lord and ask Him to help you overcome this fear. Take time to look up into the eyes of Jesus, perfect peace and then take some time to write down in your journal what comes to mind and all that the Lord has to say to you. Psalm 55 v 22[8] and 1 Peter 5 v 7[9] calls us to cast our burdens, our anxiety upon the Lord. Don't hang on to it, know that God is with you, for you and has the answer, just pour it all out to Him. See if you can feel that weight lift. This is how I took some of my own very first steps toward a God I didn't yet know, I called out for help with some problems that were threatening to tear my life apart. I was out walking, by myself, my feet felt as if my boots were made of lead and so heavy, my shoulders were slumped as if the weight of the world was crushing me into the ground. Yet as I called out, those weights did literally lift off me and a sense of lightness and hope entered my life that day.

I didn't know Him then, yet he heard me and helped me. He is Love and He loves you, just call out to Him, and He will answer you.

ROOM TO GROW.

I have come that they may have life and that they may have it more abundantly.
John 10 v 10[1] NKJV.

Everything needs room in which to grow, whether that's a plant in a pot or you as a person in your life, otherwise it, or we, becomes restricted, pot-bound and will never achieve its full potential but remain stunted. A seed that is sown will grow, put down roots and as it is doing so reach up for the light. But this seedling will soon need to be potted on and moved into a plant pot with room for its roots to grow to allow the seedling itself to grow in height and stature, whilst remaining healthy and strong. This potting on-process will require repeating, into bigger and bigger plant pots, until finally the plant is positioned in its intended place within the garden adding to and enhancing those around it. Careful attention has to be placed on its compost{growing medium}, watering and feeding regime for the whole of its life to keep it healthy and productive. The same can be said of ourselves we also need room to grow in Christ and the word of God in order to take up our positions within the Kingdom. For the King of the Kingdom, the head gardener our Father has a plan for us and a purpose which He is preparing and positioning us for. As the word of God, his truth, is sown into our hearts we have to take special care of the growing conditions. Mark 4 v 1-20[2] is the parable of the Sower and refers to four types of soil, 1/ hard, 2/stoney,3/ weedy and 4/ empty. Hard ground needs breaking up and raking to a fine tilth before seed should be sown into it. Stoney ground will need the stones removed and then also raking. Compost should be added to improve the ground and encourage the seedlings to grow. Weedy ground needs digging into and turning over, exposing the roots of the weeds and removing them, which is an ongoing process until all those invasive weed root systems have finally been eradicated. Lastly, there is a soil that is empty of anything else and is just waiting for whatever the gardener will choose to add, plants, feed, fertiliser, seeds, light and water, all are received without obstruction.

Sometimes our lives can be so hard so set and impervious to what the Lord is wanting to sow that we first need stubborn set ways breaking open in order for us to receive.

We can have that many stones, which are obstacles to correct growth, within our hearts and minds that they need removing, and raking out before anything else can be added in.

Our lives can be so full of weeds the roots of which have entwined themselves so deeply within our being that they choke the life out of anything else that is added in. Requiring the soil of our hearts to be turned upside down to expose exactly where those bitter roots live to enable full access for them to be completely removed.

Finally, we come to a place where we are open, fully open, with no resistance, readily accepting whatever it is that God is wanting to sow into our lives, from which in due time the head gardener is expecting to reap a healthy harvest. A divine holy harvest will bring Him glory but will also in the process bless us abundantly. Allow the holy spirit access to garden your heart giving you room to grow in Him.

The Gateways

1. Ask the Holy Spirit to identify areas of your life that may have become hardened and compacted or resistant to new growth, filled with stony obstacles or a bitter root that is choking out any new growth.

2. Have you remained in the same small plant pot too long and become pot-bound, stunted and unhealthy in your outlook? Ask God to give you a fresh perspective and a desire to break out of your place of restriction.

3. Ask the Lord to garden your heart and to thank him that you desire to be fruitful for him?

40

GO YOUR WAY AND EAT.

Hannah wept and would not eat.
1 Sam 1 v 7 ESV.

1 Samuel 1[1] is the story of Hannah and her desire for a son, Samuel. Hannah was one of two wives the other wife was called Peninnah. Peninnah had both sons and daughters, Hannah did not, and Peninnah, it would appear, liked to point this fact out to Hannah. Verse 6 states quite clearly that her rival used to provoke her grievously to irritate her because the Lord had closed her womb. Verse 7 shows that this was no one-off occurrence but something that went on year in, year out. "So it went on year by year as often as she, Hannah, went up to the house of the Lord, her rival would provoke her." "Therefore Hannah wept and would not eat." Her husband then asks Hannah, "Why do you weep, why do you not eat and why is your heart sad? Am I not the same to you as ten sons?" Hannah's desire, her heart's desire - verse 11 shows us what this is - is to have a child, a son.

Heartache, unfulfilled desire, and this desire of the heart brought Hannah to the house of the Lord. Each time she set out for the Lord's House would result in a constant provoking by the rival, poking, goading, and taunting her causing her to break down, weep and to stop eating.

There can be times in life where the rivals, the enemy/satan's, constant goading and provoking can bring us to a point and place of breakdown, physically, emotionally and spiritually. Where the constant stream year after year of negativity can finally cause us to break down and cease eating either physically, spiritually or both. Our hearts and minds can become so overwhelmed with fears and anxieties that we crumble. God's word says, "Keep your heart with all vigilance, for from it flow the springs of life." Proverbs 4 v 23[2]. We can hedge ourselves in with God's word, with his promises, with the truth but whenever we stop eating that hedge will grow thin in places and allow the rivals lies and taunts to enter into our hearts. Hannah comes to the house of her Lord and pours out her heart at his feet. Verse 9 after they had eaten and drunk in Shiloh Hannah rose up. Shiloh means tranquillity, rest, a place of rest. Hannah has come to a place of rest. Hannah has been held fast in bondage by the rivals' provocation for years but from a place of rest, she eats - drinks and rises up. For us to rise up we first need to come to our knees, to the house of the Lord, to the feet of our saviour and let go of strife. We need to feast upon His promises to us. Don't look back at what has been happening year upon year but keep your eyes upon the Prince of Peace. Lots wife looked back at what's been and it turned her into a pillar of salt. Life, peace and fulfilment are in the eyes of Jesus, look upon him and you won't begin to sink beneath the waves of provocation from the enemy that is coming and crashing against your life. But you will rise up in the hand of your saviour with new hope and new light in your heart. Hannah on her knees pours out her heart to the Lord and even here, one last time, she is wrongfully accused of being drunk. In verse 16 Hannah doesn't break down under the accusation but acknowledges the root cause of her heartache, anxiety and vexation. The place of peace and tranquillity is at our saviours' feet. From this position He causes us to rise up v 18. Then the woman, Hannah, went her way, ate, and her face was no longer sad. Her situation hadn't actually changed, in that she was still childless, but now the Lord has caused her to rise up and go her way, that way for her was to have a son. Went her way, ate, her face no longer sad is reflecting what's now in her heart, peace, she had laid her burden down at the Lord's feet. The provocations of the rival, are beneath her feet, behind her, they quite possibly haven't stopped but they are no longer affecting her. She is feasting in the presence of her Lord and in due time she conceived and bore Samuel who in his own due time anointed a certain shepherd boy, David, as King. When the enemy consistently provokes you, bring it all to Jesus' feet, and then rise up, feasting on all that he has for you to receive.

The Gateways

1. Hannah's pain and disappointment went on for years until eventually she broke down and poured out her heart to the Lord. If you are at this moment suffering then pour out your heart to the Lord, don't try to keep it all bottled up inside but pour it out to Him. I have taken many a walk and poured out my heart to Him as I have walked along. I've cried out to him, called out to him and I've also poured out my anger, disappointment and hurt to Him, you may as well as you can't hide your heart from him he already knows what's in there. The book of Psalms records just how David would practice this, pouring out his heart to God, it also shows us the other important thing to remember to do, which is, to praise and thank God. If you have found yourself, physically, emotionally and spiritually drained then The Lord should be the first one we look to for help. Should he prompt you to talk to someone then follow that prompting, don't ignore it.

2. Hannah's heart's desire was to have a son, God gave her, her heart's desire. What is the desire of your heart and have you given it to God?

3. There are different ways that we might come to a place of rest to eat. Walking is one. Listening to God's Word, The Bible audio through headphones is another, Christian Worship Music can help us enter into his presence. Jesus found time to be alone. The Eat part is absorbing Him inwardly, drawing on the presence of the Holy Spirit and allowing Him to strengthen you, take time to spend regular "you and God" time and allow Him to feed your soul. Then you can rise up and go your way.

41

IN DUE TIME.

The earth produces the crops on its own. First a leaf blade pushes through, then the heads of wheat are formed, and finally the grain ripens.

Mark 4 v 28[1] NLT.

And in due time, Hannah conceived and bore a son. 1 Samuel 1 v 11 records how Hannah called out, in prayer, to the Lord for a son and verse 20[2] shows the fruit of that prayer. "And in due time she {Hannah} conceived and bore a son," not a daughter or twins but exactly what she had cried out for, the desire of her heart. Her heart had been plagued with anxiety, vexation and sadness. Her desire was for a son, but take note it says "in due time," first of all Hannah conceived and then she bore a son. There was a divine answer to her prayer brought about through a natural process.

Mary the mother of Jesus, also had to go through this natural progression from conceiving to birth to receiving. Once born a babe is then given to the mother. Not even the divine birth of Jesus shortened this delivery process called, due time. Whatever it is that God has to give you has a due time and a natural progression to go through before it's placed within our arms.

First of all, comes the act of conceiving. To conceive you need to know someone intimately. We conceive the Father's will for us through an intimate relationship, knowing, with God. That which has been sown within our hearts and minds - the seeds of God's purpose for us. This will then need to move through the natural progression of growth within us. The divine will, and purpose, of God, is sown within our hearts and minds which we acknowledge and receive. Just as Mary did - she willingly received the will of God - "the" seed, and divinely conceived and walked forward with the Lord her God, trusting Him. This then allows us to go our way as we see in 1 Samuel 1 v 18, how Hannah went her way and ate and her face was no longer sad. Why? because her heart had eaten of the things of God. Cast all your cares on him. God gives us the desires of our hearts but just as with Hannah, the rival - the enemy, will come and try to steal your joy away. Joy comes in the presence of the Lord. Every time that Hannah moved towards the Lord the rival would oppose her and steal her hope her joy her expectation. On her knees, her heart poured out, her cares and worries released to the Lord, she is no longer starved but eats, receives nourishment within and goes her way no longer sad. Fear holds us, prisoner, however as 1 John 4 v 18[3] points out, "Perfect love casts out fear." His presence we eat, this is my body broken for you eat and remember. Eating of the things of God and remembering His promises, His words releases her to go her way. Her way that the Lord has for her, fulfilment of that desire, God gives us the desires of our hearts. She is walking forward released from fear, released from the provocations of the rival and free from bondage. She hasn't received yet, she hasn't actually physically received, but spiritually in her heart, she has and is no longer sad. Give it all to God, give him all those fears, and provocations, and give God access to your heart. Eat of his body his presence and walk out of sadness.

The Gateways

1. Elijah knelt down on a hilltop praying for rain to come, seven times he asked his servant, any sign yet until in due course the cloud rose up out of the sea. How do you respond to not seeing an immediate response to your prayer, give up or keep on thanking Him for what he has placed within your heart?

2. Hannah finally makes it to the Lord's house to pray and pour out her heart. Once she has done this, even though she does not possess in her hands what she had prayed for, her whole being changes. As New Testament believers we can come to the Lord anytime, anywhere, what a blessing. How do you feel in yourself when you have spent time with the Lord, Blessed, hopeful, refreshed, encouraged or.....? Ask the Holy Spirit for encouragement.

3. Have you ever sown a seed into a plant pot and watched it grow. Mark 4 v 26-29[4]. You can't have the harvest until you have been through all the stages of growth. How does waiting make you feel, frustrated, cross or expectant? Patience is a fruit of the Spirit, Galatians 5 v 22[5], and means steadfast perseverance. Thank Him that he helps, strengthens and encourages us in His fruits. Invite the Holy Spirit to help you care and nurture the seed that is sown in your heart. What Seed, Ask the Holy Spirit to show you what it is that has been sown into your heart, what He is bringing to Harvest. Journal what comes to mind.

42

ISOLATION.

Jesus took the blind man and led him out of the village. Mark 8 v 23[1] NLT

The world has been passing through a period of time where we have been told to self-isolate, to shut ourselves off from all around, which would appear to be totally contrary to Matthew 28 v 19[2] and Jesus' command to go out into all the world. God is a God of community, of family, of his people gathering together, so how can putting yourself into isolation be part of God's plan or purpose for you as an individual Child of God? The old testament talks about priests having to put themselves outside of the city gates should they touch anything unclean until they are once again clean, self-isolating themselves until clean. Anyone considered unclean had to separate themselves out from others.

In the New Testament, we see Jesus separating himself out to go up a mountain or out on a boat on the sea. Isolating himself from everything that was going on and everyone around him. Paul/Saul after the scales were removed from his eyes went out into the desert for three years. Three years out, from all that he knew as well as everyone that he had known, isolation.

We can become infected by those around us, not with some physical infection but with a spiritual malady that infects our minds, our hearts, our faith and our life. Sometimes we need to isolate ourselves. Jesus would every now and again take to the hills to refresh his mind and renew his relationship with the Father. Even though he constantly walked with the Father, he, Jesus still needed that precious time apart, isolation, to be alone with the father. Saul had to isolate himself from his old way of life completely in order to become Paul.

Sometimes we may need to isolate ourselves from a particular way of life, a friend, a group of friends or just the everyday things of daily life. Jesus took his disciples out from the everyday things so as to refresh them and renew them.

We need to be aware that there are times to isolate ourselves by putting something down, walking away from it and allowing our minds and bodies to refresh and renew before we go back and pick it up again. Our minds can become infected by something wrong that has been said or that we have read. Isolation is needed, away from this person, situation or book until we can cleanse our hearts and minds and come back in. Remaining in place and allowing the infection to increase will end up with it overflowing and inflaming all that is going on, both within you and around you. Removing ourselves out until we are cleansed and whole prevents that negative increase and overflow. Fear is such a thing, fear can spread like wildfire from one person to another as we overflow through our actions and words with panic. Strife is another, have you ever noticed how one strife-filled person can soon fill others with that same strife. Isolation, separation and renewal are required to keep our hearts and minds full and connected to our Lord.

The Gateways

1. Not that many years ago in order to get from one place to another people walked, no cars, trains etc, they just walked. It was time in which to enjoy their surroundings, to process the day, to unwind, and to pray. How often do you purposefully go out for a walk by yourself? Try to walk or simply be outside somewhere and put your mind on the things of God. Ask Him to open your eyes to His creation and give Him thanks.

2. Today we are constantly connected to the world, no matter where we are, either through our mobile phones, car radios, headphones, social media, etc. Make a point of putting them down, switching them off and isolating yourself

from it all to spend time with the Lord. Time for just Him and you, nothing else. Take time today to just sit with nothing more than your Bible, a pen and your Journal, give the Lord your attention and see what he will say to you.

3. The pressures of Church Life and Ministry can become so demanding and intense that we must make a point of regularly self-isolating from them and connecting with the Father, just as Jesus did, in order to remain refreshed and sharp. Can you see areas where you have become tired, jaded, and overwhelmed? Talk over these areas with the Father and journal what the Holy Spirit says or guides you in.

43

POWER TO HEAL.

The power of the Lord was with him to heal.
Luke 5 v 17 ESV.

And the power of the Lord was with him to heal Luke 5 v 17[1]. With whom? Well, the power of the Lord was with Jesus.

This is Jesus the son of God. We can read just a few verses earlier in Luke 4 v 40[2] where it states that "All those who had any who were sick with various diseases brought them to him, and he laid hands on every one of them and he healed them all." He, Jesus, then continues over the following scriptures to heal people.

So Jesus, who is healing people from all sorts of things as well as casting out demons, comes to a place or a position, in which, he is now teaching as we can read in Luke 5 v 17[3], "On one of these days, as He was teaching." Yet as we continue to read further, the verse goes on to say, "The power of the Lord was with him." He the Lord, the son of God, is here described as having, at this time, the power of the Lord with him to heal. Jesus, the Lord, through the power of the Lord is being moved/guided/directed, specifically, to heal. Jesus healed in many different ways, he did nothing outside of the Father's will, John 5 v 19. He lived by always being in constant communion with Him, the Father, through the Holy Spirit, the power of God. The Holy Spirit is described as the power of God, Ephesians 3 v 16-20. Here, in Luke 5v17, we see that the power of God was with him, Jesus, to heal. The direction here is to heal, not teach, but to heal. Now Jesus did nothing in his own will. Teaching was part of his ministry calling, to open blind eyes and deaf ears, literally in healing but also in teaching to the things of God. So he is teaching as directed by the Father, but now that direction moves and here Jesus is being guided specifically to heal.

Jesus was busy teaching to a packed house when suddenly, the roof above Him was literally opened up and His focus was shifted from teaching to healing, as a sick man on a bed was lowered down in front of His eyes. Yet through that act of healing the sick man, He continued to open locked minds and teach as we see in Luke 5 v 26[4] "And amazement seized them all, and they glorified God and were filled with awe, saying, "We have seen extraordinary things today."

There are times in our own walk where guidance from the Spirit will come upon us to heal specifically a person a disease or a situation. We may be very busy with some other ministry activity, such as teaching, or reading out our well-prepared notes, yet in the midst of doing so comes the guidance from the Holy Spirit to heal, to cease from our original intent, purpose, and to move our focus upon healing. To be able to do this and respond involves a relationship, just as Jesus had which he says we also have, we need to be aware of and walk in his guidance. Don't forget he is the Lord and not us so listen to that prompting and respond. So that the roof above you opens up and allows the power of God to flow freely and not for the said roof to cave in on you as you stubbornly continue in your own way. Be open at all times to the things of God and the Holy Spirit. The Spirit of the Lord God is upon me to ..... do whatever he says Isaiah 61.

The Gateways

1. The children's rhyme, sticks and stones may break my bones but words can never hurt me, we all know this to be untrue. Our words contain the power to build someone up or to tear them down, Ephesians 4 v 29 directs us to speak words of encouragement to build up. Our spoken words can bring healing to someone or they can inflame a situation. Why do you think it's important to listen for God's words in any situation that we may find ourselves in.

2. When you are busy about something and the Holy Spirit prompts you to do something else, how would you respond, positively to the Holy Spirit or press on with what you're doing.

3. Have you encountered the presence of the Holy Spirit prompting you, if you have not been aware of Him, take some time to sit quietly and ask for the Holy Spirit to teach you and guide you, journal what comes in your heart and mind. Thank him that He is your teacher, counsellor and guide. John 14 v 26

44

RENEWAL.

Do not be conformed to this world but be transformed by the renewal of your mind Romans 12 v 2 ESV.?

Romans 12 v 2[1] says "*Do not be conformed to this world but be transformed by the renewal of your mind, that by testing you may discern what is the will of God, what is good and acceptable and perfect.*"

Renewal comes from the Greek word anakainosis[2], Strongs G342, which means - renewal, renovation, complete change for the better - effected by the Holy Spirit.

Complete change for the better, allowing the Holy Spirit to change our minds and our viewpoint, on something, is a power for good. Which will help us to see the good, acceptable and perfect will of God. Wow yes, please.

In Titus 3 v 5[3] we read. "*He saved us not because of works done by us in righteousness but according to his own mercy by the washing of regeneration and renewal of the Holy Spirit.*" The word "Regeneration," palingenesia[4] here means - production of a new life consecrated to God, as through Spiritual rebirth. We not only have our minds renewed but are also washed by the Holy Spirit. Have you ever felt regenerated and refreshed by your morning shower? Yes. Well, it is nothing compared to what comes through the washing of The Holy Spirit, that brings forth New Life. First thing in the morning as the sun rises, nighttime ends and a new day begins. This whole picture of rebirth comes through the renewing power of the Holy Spirit, cleansing us, washing us, fresh and new.

Renewal of the mind is a moving of position from death to life, darkness to light, from ignorance to understanding, and from separation to connection. Renewal is an opening up of the mind to receive fresh insight, new revelation knowledge, and connection to the things of God. In Hosea 4 v 6[5] we hear God's cry "My people are destroyed for a lack of knowledge." The word destroyed, dama,[6] means, cut off, cease. A lack of knowledge causes us to be cut off, separated, to cease. It is a place of darkness without knowledge and we can find ourselves living in a state of death, separation from the well of life, cut off. Jesus opened up their minds to understand the scriptures Luke 24 v 45[7]. Opening our minds to the truth is a rolling away of the stone of isolation, that is in front of the tomb. Removal of that stone allowed Lazarus to walk forwards from death to life from darkness into light as the Lord called him forth in life, Renewal. There was opposition to this action as the traditions of man and our own experience or knowledge were contrary to what Jesus said and would otherwise keep that door shut. But renewal comes through the work of the Holy Spirit the power of God. The Holy Spirit recalls things to our minds for us to meditate on, inquire about and receive teaching, wisdom, knowledge, revelation and renewal upon. All of this leads us out of the tomb of darkness, ignorance, death, or something in which we are dead to the truth and leads us forth into light, understanding and life. Knowledge of the things of God is light. Jesus is the Word of God who is the Light and the Life. Through renewal, we receive or undergo a complete change for the better. This kind of renewal changes our lives forever bringing about new life growth and a greater depth of relationship with the Trinity. Changes like this can be met with opposition and resistance such as the tombstone blocking the way, the ways of the world which lead to death or perhaps even coming from the traditions of our own family. Be not conformed to it, Jesus said fear not for I have overcome the world. Jesus put death beneath his feet and made a way for us to move from death to life, from darkness to light, from fear to peace. Allow the Holy Spirit to work on your heart and mind and bring about a complete life-changing renewal. Listen and grow.

The Gateways

1. In Judges 6 v 25-27 Gideon is called by the Angel of the Lord to pull down the altar that his father had built and is then given instructions on how to build an altar to God properly, in the ordered way. Are you carrying around a way of doing something, a tradition of your fathers that needs pulling down and removing so that the Lord can show you how to do it His way?

2. Luke 24 v 45 We saw how the disciples were struggling and needed help to understand the parables, so they asked their Lord for help. Jesus responded by opening up the disciples' minds for them so that they might understand. Are there scriptures that you are struggling to understand? Spend time with the Lord and ask for him to open up your mind and help you understand, to give you revelation. To renew your mind.

3. Do you feel frightened by Renewal? Does the thought of stepping forward in faith cause you to doubt and fear? Are you fastened in by the tombstone of routine and tradition? Ask the Lord for help to see the Light that he is shining for you to follow and walk forward into. Ask him to renew your outlook as He calls your name and invites you to come out of the darkness.

45

SEPARATING.

And God saw that the light was good, and he separated the light from the darkness.
Genesis 1 v 4[1] ESV.

Separate or the act of causing something to be separate from something else takes place right at the beginning of the Bible in Genesis chapter one. Where we see God causing the light to be separate from the darkness and that it was good. This separation was good, it was a good thing to do.

Separate:- badal[2], means to disjoin, as two places by a veil, fence, wall, things that were, previously, mixed together.

Separating:- nazar[3], means to set apart for sacred duties, consecrate, separating self.

From the beginning, we can also see how the enemy has gone all out to separate us from the closeness and knowledge of our Father and is still to this day trying to keep us, God's children, separate from the knowledge of who we are and the close companionship with our God. Needless to say this kind of separate is not a good thing or position to be in.

Close companionship, with our Father God, is our rightful place in which to be. God through the work of the cross brings back together that which has been separated out by the work of the enemy. Separate from the fullness of God by the lies of the enemy. Deceit caused us to be cast out from the fullness of God's presence in the Garden of Eden. We were created to exist fully in his presence, to live fully in the rarefied atmosphere of the presence of the Father. Outside of that, we exist by his good grace and by the work of the cross we can through the invitation of Jesus and by the power of the Holy Spirit move back into that very presence of our Father God.

The enemy will come through lies, deceit, and temptations to entice us out of that position. As long as we are misled, guided, or directed by any lies of the enemy and we move our eyes even if only briefly away from the true light, that moment can open up a doorway. "For where envying and strife is, there is confusion and every evil work." James 3 v 16[4].

As long as we continue to walk in this position of deceit we can find ourselves in a place separate from the truth, disjoined by a veil, a fence, a wall from the things that were previously mixed together, putting us into disunity. By opening our hearts and minds to the work of the Holy Spirit who is our teacher and is always pointing us toward the truth, that disjoined separate is replaced by a separating, a consecrating, a setting apart of oneself to the truth and a removing of the lie. Replacing the lie for truth or death for life brings light to our whatever it may have been that was dark. As we look to our Lord we will find truth, light, guidance and direction, putting us back into a position of unity. Our minds as in Romans 12 v 2 will be renewed and we will walk forwards in Light, growing in the wisdom stature and knowledge of the things of God. Do not be conformed to this world, but be transformed by the renewal of your mind, that by testing you may discern what is the will of God, what is good and acceptable and perfect. Keep your eyes and your mind on the Truth.

The Gateways

1. In Joshua 3, the people had to Sanctify themselves before they could cross the Jordan and enter into the Promised Land and into all that God had promised them. Sanctify also means to separate oneself as seen above. The people were separating themselves from a way of life they had walked for forty years, preparing themselves to enter into a new way of life in the Promised Land. Are there things that you need to separate yourself from, such as an old way of life, in order to allow you to move forward with the Lord? Take time to ask Him and then journal what He has to say or that which he reveals to you.

2. Romans 12 v 2, transformed by the renewing of your mind means, change the way you think. Ask the Lord to show you areas in which you need to change the way you think. Journal what He shows you and then ask him for His help to renew your mind.

3. Perhaps there are areas in which the enemy is deceiving, lying or tempting you. Ask the Holy Spirit to reveal any part of your life in which the enemy has a toehold. Thank the Lord that He is a God of truth and that He has already defeated satan at the cross. Thank Him that he will help you walk away from any darkness that may have crept into your life.

46

GATHERED INTO THE ARK. GENESIS 6.

But I will establish my covenant with you, and you shall come into the ark, you, your sons, your wife, and your sons wives with you. GENESIS 6. v 18[1] ESV.

A storm is coming, a flood, all life as you know it is about to change, that which was is about to cease and make way for that which is to come. The end of the old ways and the beginning of the new.

Now I am giving you instructions to build a vessel that will carry you through this storm. Store up within it all that you need to feed yourself and your family through this storm. Then God sealed them in. Everything they needed to keep them alive had to have already been stored up previously within the vessel, the Ark. Once the storm came and the door had been sealed shut, nothing else could be added. They were sealed in until the storm had ceased, the flood waters had receded and they had been released to stand on dry ground. Even then, after they had stood on the dry ground, they would have to go through a season of relying upon their stores whilst the seeds that they had carried with them, were sown into the ground beneath their feet and had time to grow and produce a harvest.

This was a direct warning to Noah about something catastrophic that was about to happen and how God intended to provide a way through it for him and his family. All that was needed was faith and the appropriate obedient action.

God supplies us with all that we need and it is up to us to take a hold of it, receive it, and store it up within for future use. When something like the flood hits us and our world comes crashing down or is swept away, all we have to stand on is the promises of God. Those promises that we have received from him, taken in, written down and engraved within our hearts and minds, stored up for future use. These personal God-given words are what we will need to feed on, to encourage and strengthen ourselves with. This storehouse is what we will need to keep returning to, over and over again. It is the storehouse of God's truth that will pick us up when the long dark storm-filled days drag on and become weeks, months, and perhaps years, Noah and his family were shut up in the Ark for over a year.

These long dark times are horrible, they are not nice. "These things I have spoken unto you, that in me ye might have peace. In the world ye shall have tribulation: but be of good cheer; I have overcome the world."John 16v33. God is our deliverer and his word, his promises are true. Hold fast to him and feed yourself daily, do not cease from praying and keep your eyes focused on Jesus who is the way the truth and the life.

Make sure your vessel, your heart, is full of truth. In the book of Ruth, we can see how Ruth herself, ate at Boaz's table whilst Naomi, her mother-in-law, sat at home with nothing, hungry. Ruth fed herself until her hunger was satiated, then once she had eaten her fill, went home and took with her food from her provider's table with which to feed Naomi. These two women had just been through a life-changing storm of their own.

Make sure you feed well at your provider's table, God's table so that in turn you have enough to be able to feed others that are desperately hungry and in need of sustenance.

The Gateways

1. Noah's obedience to God and by listening to and acting accordingly delivered himself and his family safely. If he had listened to the World's opinion, around him, then we wouldn't be talking about Noah. Can you see areas where you have received God's guidance and areas where you have chosen to believe others' opinions? Ask The Lord to show you where you have chosen the World's ways above His. Repent and ask Him for help to choose His way.

2. We can read how Mary and Joseph were warned to flee to Egypt and how the three Wise Men were also warned not to return to Herod but to go home a different way. Is God still warning us today about problems, and troubles that lie ahead and how to deal with them, avoid them or deliver us through them? Is God warning you of up-and-coming problems? Thank Him that He is our deliverer and leads us.

3. When someone needs help what overflows from your heart, God's love or worldly advice? What have you been feeding on and storing up as that is what will overflow? Ask the Lord to show you what your heart is full of.

47

STAY AWAKE - KEEP WATCH.

And what I say to you I say to all, stay awake Mark 13 v 37[1] ESV.

Mark 13 v 37[1]. "And what I say to you I say to all "Stay awake."" Jesus is talking not only to the disciples gathered close by but this is also a call of His that echoes down through the ages to all of us who sit before Him. This is not just a simple suggestion of Jesus but a command, a direction for us all to pay attention. "Stay awake."

In the Greek:-gregoreo[2], 'Awake,' means:- To watch, give strict attention to, be cautious, active to take heed lest, through remissness and indolence, some destructive calamity suddenly overtakes one.

This last part of the meaning, "To take active heed," lays the responsibility squarely with us and it is well worth taking a look at the two words that follow on from heed, "Remissness" and "Indolence". What do these words actually mean?

Remiss means to be negligent and lacking care.

Indolence means, avoidance of activity or exertion, laziness.

These two words describe or warn us of how we might not take active heed of the things of God or what He is saying to us.

It is important, for us, to keep our eyes on Jesus, to remain vigilant about our relationship with the Triune God. When we become lethargic towards our time with God, negligent and lacking care about spending time with Him and grow lazy, "*indolent,*" in our relationship, then we are in danger of falling asleep to His precious life-giving power.

Life itself can be demanding, Luke 8 v 14 warns us that worldly life can choke out the things of God. There is no way that we can flourish in the things of God, without the Lord's help. Our call is to stay awake and pay attention to our time with the Lord, it is a time of refreshing and strengthening for the day ahead. Jesus Himself was becoming overcome with the cares and worries of this world, that which was in front of Him was causing Him stress, fear and anxiety. He had come into the garden, separated Himself from the disciples, to spend time with the Father and bringing it all before Him. He knew what lay ahead, He knew what had to be done. Three times Jesus asked for this cup to be taken away from Himself, and three times He said not my will but yours be done. Even though He, Jesus, sweated blood through it He remained awake to the things of God, the will of God, His Father. Habakkuk in Habakkuk 2 v 1 -2 climbed up to his watchtower to see what the Lord would say to him, he was standing watch, waiting. He was upset about things and called out to see what He the Lord would say to him. He was staying awake to God, staying awake to the things of God. In this verse the word watch means, to watch closely, lean forward and peer into. In v 2 the Lord answers him.

When things get busy or overwhelming it is so easy to just put our time with the Lord to one side, to shelve Him, so to speak. We need to make sure that we stay awake to the things of God, to our need to watch and see what he would say to us. To make time to fix our eyes on the things above on that which God is revealing to us and remember, this day, to stay awake. Rise up O sleeper and live. Stay Awake don't get remiss, don't get lazy.

The Gateways

1. How might we stay awake to the things of God? Do you think it simply means reading more of the Bible or is it suggesting something else? If so what might that be? How do you think we might become lazy to our time spent with the Lord?

2. Habakkuk set himself to see what God might say. How do you engage with the Lord? Why is it important to set yourself? The word "Set" means position. He set himself to see what God might say to him, it is important to wait on Him for His answer. Do you wait or move on to something else?

3. Are there things in your life, your day that is drawing you away from staying awake to God, that is demanding your time, your energy and your attention? Ask God to open your eyes to Him, so that you might hear what He is saying to you. Ask Him to help you ascertain what is important right now and needs retaining and what, on the other hand, is not and should be let go of. God will help you to prioritise and bring order out of what may be overwhelming you.

1 Peter 5 v 7 - 8[3] says. "Casting all your anxieties on Him, because He cares for you. Be sober-minded, *be watchful.*

48

STAY AWAKE - REMAIN VIGILANT.

Be sober, be vigilant because your adversary the devil walks about like a roaring lion, seeking whom he may devour. 1 Pet 5 v 8[1] NKJV.

Are you called? Yes, if you believe in the Lord you are "called" according to His purposes, Romans 8 v 28[2] "And we know that all things work together for good to them that love God, to them who are the called according to *his* purpose." We are called according to His plans and purposes for your life, not your plans and purposes but God's. "A man's heart plans his way, but the LORD directs his steps.' Proverbs 16 v 9[3]

You have a plan and a purpose and the Holy Spirit is leading you forth in that. Hopefully, we respond and walk with him. However, the cares and concerns of this life can become overwhelming, demanding of your time and attention. We may find ourselves despairing and fearful of the future and what it may hold for us. We may even lose sight of God's plan and God's purpose and we may prefer to go our way and do things differently.

Jesus, yes Jesus, was in such a position in the garden of Gethsemane[4]. He was fearful and sweating blood, He was asking His Father for His future to be changed, yet being aware of the deceptiveness of the flesh and remaining awake to the things of God. Fear was trying to overcome Jesus, fear of the future and what lay before Him. The Son - Jesus - God with us, is bowing the knee to His Father, God in heaven, and declaring "Yet not my will but yours be done." Why? For the Glory of God that was set before Him.

God's plan and God's purpose are for His Glory that is set before us. God's plan and purpose for your life is for the revelation of God's glory through you in whichever way that may be. It may be by speaking to someone you might not want to, it may be missionary work, it may be ….. whatever it is that he has put in your heart to do. Stay awake to his plans. Remain vigilant and watchful for the works of the enemy, the tempter, trying to draw you away from it. Lean into the things of God - remain vigilant.

Some of Jesus's very last words to his disciples in the garden before he died upon the cross were, stay awake.

The Gateways

1. Do you feel in your time of need that you have been left and are on your own? All those in the garden with Jesus kept falling asleep, unable to support and assist Him. Jesus fell on his knees before His Father. Turn your eyes on the Lord and fix your mind upon the One who died for you. Thank Him for all that He did and is still doing for you. Make a list of who Jesus is to you and thank Him for each one as it comes to mind. He is my deliverer, thank you Lord that "You are my deliverer".

2. Take each one of the things you have written down, go over it and expand on it. He is my deliverer, what does that mean to you? He will see me safe through this storm, through this dark time.

3. Thank the Lord that you are not here by accident and for no reason. You are here, in such a time as this, for God's specific plans and purposes for your life and that He will help you. Ask Him to refresh your mind on what and where He is leading you at this moment, however big or small it may be.

49

STAY AWAKE - REMAIN FOCUSED.

John the baptist asking. "Are you the one who is to come, or shall we look for another?" Matthew 11 v 3[1] ESV.

God gives us visions, indicators of what He is calling us to do. We can see records of this right through the Bible. We can read how Noah received directions - instructions on how to build an Ark. An Ark in which Noah and his family, along with all the different kinds of life that lived on the Earth would be saved and delivered through a terrible storm. All the way through the Bible, record after record we can continue to read, right through to the New Testament and the Apostles, such as Saul {Paul} and his revelation from the Lord as he met with Him on the road to Damascus. There are more such encounters written down all the way to the very last book, Revelation in which we hear about John's testimony of all that he was told in the heavenly realms.

From there onwards we can pick books up and read of the visions and dreams that other folks have received from the Lord right through to the present day. God never changes and He will always be revealing His plans and purposes to individuals like you and me.

Sometimes these dreams, visions, and plans, can come to pass fairly quickly, other times they may take longer, and some may even take a lifetime. Whilst certain visions may be something that you are putting into place for others that follow to complete. Think about David, the plans for the Temple of God and David's son Solomon.

Many years ago the Lord gave me a vision, a plan and a purpose. He showed me something that I believe I have pursued wholeheartedly ever since and as far as I am aware it has not yet come to pass, not fully. This path has been painful, costly and hard. I have repeatedly asked him if it's right if it is the right path, did I actually hear Him correctly, should I go and do something else instead. The first recorded doubt is in Genesis where the serpent, Satan, questions Eve with "Did God say." The enemy is still in the business of sowing the seeds of doubt into our minds today. Every time I have experienced those seeds of doubt I have taken them to the Lord and asked Him. There have been times when I have been slow to seek Him. God never changes and His replies have always pointed me back to the truth, to what He had said, what He had revealed to me. His replies always contain the very same message, relating back to or are connected with the original verses and guidance that He gave me. Each time revealing it in a different way, yet each time encouraging me, pointing me towards His plan and purpose, strengthening me to press on, to keep my eyes on Him and to wait. To stay awake to the things of God, to keep myself sharp, to soak myself in Him. In this, there is hope that certain, as yet unfulfilled, promises that he has made to us will come to pass. I could focus on the struggles, sometimes I do, but He calls us to "remember the good that He's done." There have been along this path, many wonderful times with my Lord that we have experienced and encountered that are, quite simply, beyond price. Moments to treasure, rejoice in and give thanks for as we continue to move forward. These encounters that we have experienced just keep you coming back to Him for more and more of Him. For a deeper and closer relationship with our Father.

Psalm 84 v 10[2] puts it this way, "Better is one day in your courts than a thousand elsewhere." If we desire to see more of our God, to go deeper with Him then we need to, "Stay Awake," to the things of God, to remain focused on Him, to the race that is set before us, to His plans and purposes. Listen out for the still small voice that is speaking out encouragement to you. Stay awake and remain watchful, remain focused.

The Gateways

1. Everybody's walk, plan, or purpose is different from someone else's. Paul encourages us to run the race that is set before you. It is for us to stay awake to the things of God, to that which He has called you to. How might you do that?

2. What is it that keeps you coming back to God for more of Him? Do you want more of Him? Do you have a desire within your heart to know your God more deeply?

3. Journaling the Things of God, those that He has revealed to me over the years has helped me to Stay Awake to them, to be watchful for them and desire them. Go back over the things that the Lord may have revealed to you as you have gone through this book with Him, pray over them and see what else He has to say to you. How have they affected you? If God has revealed things to you then it is good to Stay Awake to them and not be remiss or indolent.

50

LOCKDOWN.

The doors being locked where the disciples were for fear of … John 20 v 19[1] ESV.

Lockdown is a word that will, quite possibly, always be associated with the year 2020 as the Covid virus swept across the globe changing people's perceptions and lives forever. Yet lockdown is not something new, as the preacher says in Ecclesiastes 1 v 9[2] "There is nothing new under the sun." Lockdown has occurred throughout the Bible, from start to finish, in many different forms and places. Starting in the Book of Genesis, chapter 6, with Noah and his family, God shut them in and sealed up the door behind them once they had all set foot inside of the Ark. They found themselves in a place of "Lockdown" for over a year as they were safely transported to a new life and a new beginning, they had been separated out from all that was taking place around them. Noah and his family were delivered through darkness and storm.

Many old testament cities found themselves in a state of lockdown, the gateways closed and barred as the people within endured as opposing forces laid siege to them, looking for a way to get in. The people who had been going about their daily business suddenly found themselves besieged by the enemy. These folks within would be looking for a breakthrough and release from the lockdown situation that they had found themselves in.

Jonah, locked down in the belly of the fish, not what he had expected or planned for, but the graciousness of God delivered him from his own stubbornness, via that fish's, smelly stomach, to a land where thousands of people were about to have their lives changed from death to Life as Jonah brought the Word of God to their shores. This man of God found himself somewhere frightening and very dark until he called out to his Lord for help.

Another man of God was marching zealously forward, yet remained blind to the truth of the Lord Jesus Christ. Saul, after an encounter with Jesus, became Paul through the lockdown of blindness, released into a new way of seeing and as a result Gentile folks, such as myself, have been added into God's family.

The Apostle Paul, from a position of lockdown within the city of Rome, wrote letters of teaching and encouragement to the different churches that he had visited. Paul, who was physically unable to walk out of his captivity wrote his letters of encouragement which, for us, today, make up a great portion of the New Testament and bring freedom to many.

Following the death of their Lord on the Cross the disciples were in lockdown in a house in the town, the doors and windows were shut and barred to those outside. The disciples were fearful and frightened of what may happen to them, they were shut up, feeling lost and alone.

They were locked down through fear, unable to face the people who were outside those four walls, until the resurrected Jesus walked right through those opposing walls entering into the very midst of them, and then walking them out of those fears.

A group of disciples were guided to an upper room by the words of Jesus himself, where they were to remain, in lockdown, until the power of the Holy Spirit came upon them and changed them completely. Approximately 1 out of 4 of the followers of Jesus Christ actually listened to what he said and did what He said. Out of the 500[1] that should have listened and obeyed the lockdown guidance given to them by Jesus-remain in the room, only 120 followed what He had said to do. As those 120 emerged from that upper room experience, filled with the Holy Spirit, people from all nations were gathered together outside, 3000 of these folks gave their lives to Christ as those disciples preached the message of Good News.

The Gateways.

1. As you read through the above examples how did they resonate with your spirit? Pray over them and journal what the Lord has to say to you through them.

2. The negative sides of lockdown can keep us bound up in darkness and fear, seek the Lord's help and guidance to walk you out of this captivity and into freedom.

3. Have you experienced any positive fruits from a period of lockdown? List them, giving God thanks for the good fruits you have received.

SCRIPTURE REFERENCES

1. ALWAYS TRUE. 1. Nehemiah Ch 9v7-8 NLT. 2. John Ch 1v5 NIV. 3. 1Samuel Ch 30v6 ESV. 4. John Ch 16V24 ESV. 5.1 Samuel Ch 30v8 ESV. 6. 1 Samuel Ch 30v17-19 KJV. 7. Matthew Ch 12v20 ESV. 8. Isaiah Ch 42v3 ESV. 9. Strongs G2920 Blue Letter Bible. 10. Strongs G1544 Blue Letter Bible. 11. Strongs G3534 Blue Letter Bible. 12. Nehemiah Ch.9v8 NLT

2. A New Year A New Perspective.

1. Isaiah Ch 35v10 ESV. 2. Isaiah Ch 43v19 ESV.

3. Morning Glory.

1. Psalm Ch 30v5 ESV. 2. John Ch 21v4-14 ESV.

3. John Ch 21v 12-13 ESV. 4. John Ch 21v15-17 ESV.

4. The Honking Of The Geese.

1. Hebrews13v5 NKJV. 2. Psalm Ch 50v15 ESV. 3. 2 Samuel Ch 22v4 NIV. 4. John Ch 14v26 ESV. 5. 2 Kings Ch 6v17 ESV.

5. FIRST STEPS.

1. John Ch 11v 9 ESV. 2. Romans Ch 14v13 ESV. 3. Philippians Ch 4v8 ESV. 4. John Ch 11v39. KJV.

6. WHEN GOD CALLS.

1. Genesis Ch 1v3 ESV. 2. John Ch 8v12 ESV. 3. John Ch 9v5 ESV. 4. John Ch 11v9 ESV. 5. Matthew Ch 4v18 - 22.

7. WE ARE NOT ALONE.

1. John Ch 14v23 ESV.

8. A CLOVE OF GARLIC.

1. John Ch10v10 ESV. 2. Isaiah Ch 55v10-11. ESV. 3. Luke Ch 23v44ESV.

9. IN ORDER TO SEE WE MUST FIRST HEAR.

1. Ephesians Ch1v18 ESV. 2. Genesis Ch1v1-2 ESV. 3. Ezekiel Ch 47v6 KJV. 4.

10. SEATED WITH CHRIST.

1. Ephesians Ch2v6 NLT. 2. Galatians Ch 2v20 ESV.

11. THIS IS THE DAY THAT THE LORD HAS MADE.

1. Psalm Ch 118v24 ESV. 2. Psalm Ch 118v24 NKJV.

12. <u>STAND ON IT, OR HOW TO RECEIVE SOMETHING GIVEN TO YOU BY GOD.</u>

1. Joshua Ch 1v3 ESV. 2. Genesis Ch 13v14-15/17 ESV.

13. <u>CAN I BORROW THE PENCIL SHARPENER?</u>

1. Matthew Ch 7v7 ESV.

14. <u>RECOGNISING FALSE DIRECTIONS.</u>

1. Colossians Ch 3v15 KJV.

15. <u>EXPLORING YOUR THOUGHTS.</u>

1. 2 Corinthians Ch 10v5 ESV. 2. Matthew Ch 3v3 KJV. 3. 2 Corinthians Ch 10v4-5 ESV. 4. James Ch 1v17 ESV. 5. 1 Timothy Ch 4v15 NKJV.

16. <u>STORMS.</u>

1. Matthew Ch 14v24 NLT. 2. Matthew Ch 14v24 ESV. 3. Joshua Ch1v5 ESV. 4. Hebrews Ch 13v5 ESV. 5. John Ch 16v33 ESV.

17. <u>BUILDING AN ALTAR.</u>

1. Genesis Ch 8v20 ESV. 2. Genesis Ch 8v21 Amplified Bible Compact Edition 1987. 3. Revelation Ch12v11 NKJV.

18. <u>ANCHORS.</u>

1. Hebrews Ch 6v19 ESV. 2. Hebrews Ch 6v19 Amplified Bible Compact Edition 1987. 3. Strongs G5590, psyche. Blue Letter Bible. 4. Jeremiah Ch 31v17 ESV. 5. Jeremiah Ch 29v11 ESV.

19. <u>GATEWAYS.</u>

1. John Ch 14v6 ESV.

20. <u>A PLAN AND A PURPOSE.</u>

1. Esther Ch 4v14. 2. Jeremiah Ch 29v11 ESV. 3. 1 Chronicles Ch 28v12 NIV. 4. Habakkuk Ch 2v2 ESV. 5. Joshua Ch 7v3 ESV. 6. Joshua Ch 8v1 ESV.

21. <u>EVERYTHING UNDER CONTROL.</u>

1. Luke Ch 22v42 ESV.

22. <u>TAKING A SNAPSHOT.</u>

1. Ezekiel Ch 40v4 ESV. 2. 1 Corinthians Ch 11v24 ESV. 3. Philippians Ch 4v8 ESV.

23. <u>DEVOTED TO DESTRUCTION</u>

1. Romans Ch 12v9 ESV. 2. Joshua Ch 1v11 ESV. 3. Strongs H 3423 Blue Letter Bible. 4. Joshua Ch 6v5 ESV. 5. Joshua Ch 10v39 ESV. 6. Romans Ch12v9 ESV. 7. 2 Corinthians Ch 10v5 ESV.

24. <u>IT'S IN THE DETAIL.</u>

1. Luke Ch 2v20 NIV.

25. <u>A NUT OF HOPE, A LIGHT IN THE DARKNESS.</u>

1. Psalm Ch 42v5 NIV.

26. <u>ADMITTING THAT YOUR WRONG.</u>

1. Isaiah Ch 30v21 ESV. 2. Luke Ch 23v24 ?? 3. Proverbs Ch 16v18 ESV. 4. Isaiah Ch 30v21 ESV. 5. Acts Ch 10v15 NLT.

27. <u>THE RIVER OF LIFE.</u>

1. Ezekiel Ch 47v8 NLT. 2. Revelation Ch 22v1 Amplified Bible Compact Edition 1987. 3. Ezekiel Ch 47v6 ESV.

28. <u>THE ONLY TRUE GOD.</u>

1. Exodus Ch 3v13-14 ESV. 2. 1 Kings Ch 18v27 ESV.

29. <u>HEALING.</u>

1. James Ch 1v17 ESV. 2. James Ch 1v17 ESV. 3. Romans Ch 8v28 ESV. 4. Mark Ch 9v24 ESV. 5. Mark Ch 9v24 Amplified Bible Compact Edition 1987. 6. Isaiah Ch 60v1 Amplified Bible Compact Edition 1987. 7. 1 Peter Ch 2v24 ESV.

30. <u>DESIRING TO DO GOOD.</u>

1. Deuteronomy Ch 30v19 ESV. 2. John Ch 14v6 NKJV. 3. Shine. Strongs H215, or, Blue Letter Bible.

31. <u>A PROPHECY OR A PROMISE? SPOKEN AND GIVEN.</u>

1. Joshua Ch 23v14 NLT. 2. 1 Kings Ch 17-18 ESV. 3. 2 Corinthians Ch 1v20 NLT. 4. Joshua Ch 23v14 ESV. 5. Acts Ch 23v11 ESV. 6. Acts Ch 27v23-26 ESV.

32. <u>ARISE EAT AND DRINK.</u>

1. 1 Kings Ch 19v7 ESV. 2. Beersheba, Strongs H884, Blue Letter Bible. 3. 1Kings Ch 19v4 ESV. 4. Kings Ch 19v5-8 ESV. 5. Psalm 23v5 ESV. 6. Strongs H7979. Blue Letter Bible.

33. <u>LIVING IN THE HOUSE OF GOD.</u>

1. Genesis Ch 2v7 KJV. 2. John Ch 14v20-26 ESV. 3. Ephesians Ch 2v19 ESV.

34. <u>WALKING FORWARDS INTO FREEDOM.</u>

1. Philippians Ch 3v14 ESV. 2. 2 Chronicles Ch 20v21 ESV. 3. John Ch 11v44 ESV. 4 Matthew Ch 14v23 ESV. 5. Genesis Ch 12v1. 6. Galatians Ch 1v11-20 ESV. 7. Philippians Ch 3v13-14. 8. Joshua Ch 22v4-6.

35. <u>THEN HE SHOWED ME.</u>

1. Exodus Ch 14v13 KJV. 2. Revelation Ch 22v1 ESV. 3. Matthew Ch 13v11 ESV. 4. Ezekiel Ch 47v6. ESV. 5. Revelation Ch 4v1. ESV. 6. Mark Ch3v13 ESV. 7. Exodus Ch 14v13 ESV. 8. John 4v35 ESV. 9. Luke Ch 5v4 ESV. 10. Luke Ch 24v45 ESV. 11. Psalm 119v105 ESV.

36. LEARNING TO LOVE.

1. Matthew Ch 22v37 ESV. 2. Matthew 22v39 ESV. 3. Galatians 2v20 ESV. 4. Proverbs 16v9 NKJV.

37. LEST THEY FEINT ON THE WAY.

1. Matthew Ch 15v32 ESV. 2. Isaiah Ch 42v3 ESV. 3. Matthew Ch 15v32-39 ESV. 4. Ruth 2v18.

38. THIS IS MY BELOVED SON.

1. Matthew Ch 17v5 ESV. 2. John Ch 14v26. 3. Strongs G3339 metamorphoo. 4. Matthew Ch 17v7. 5. 1 John Ch 4v18 ESV. 6. Matthew Ch 17v1 ESV. 7. 2 Corinthians Ch 5V17 ESV. 8. Psalm 55v22 ESV. 9. 1 Peter Ch 5v7 ESV.

39. ROOM TO GROW.

1. John Ch 10v10 NKJV. 2. Mark Ch 4v1-20 ESV..

40. GO YOUR WAY AND EAT.

1. 1 Samuel Ch 1v1-20 ESV. 2. Proverbs 4v23 ESV.

41. IN DUE TIME.

1. Mark Ch 4v28 NLT. 2. 1 Samuel Ch 1v20 ESV. 3. 1 John Ch 4v18 ESV. 4. Mark Ch 4v26-29 ESV. 5. Galatians Ch 5v22 ESV.

42. ISOLATION.

1. Mark Ch 8v23 NLT. 2. Matthew Ch 28v19 ESV.

43. POWER TO HEAL.

1. Luke Ch 5v17 ESV. 2. Luke Ch 4v40 ESV. 3. Luke Ch 5v17 ESV. 4.Luke Ch 5v26 ESV.

44. RENEWAL.

1. Romans Ch 12v2 ESV. 2. Strongs G342, anakainosis, Blue Letter Bible. 3. Titus Ch 3v5 ESV. 4. Strongs G3824, palingenesia, Blue Letter Bible. 5. Hosea Ch 4v6 ESV. 6. Strongs H1820 dama, Blue Letter Bible. 7. Luke Ch 24v45 ESV.

45. SEPARATING.

1. Genesis Ch 1v4 ESV. 2. Strongs H914, badal, Blue Letter Bible. 3. Strongs H5144 nazar, Blue Letter Bible. 4. James Ch 3v16 KJV.

46. GATHERED INTO THE ARK. GENESIS 6.

1. Genesis Ch 6v18 ESV. 2. John Ch 16v33 KJV.

47. STAY AWAKE - KEEP WATCH.

1. Mark Ch 13v37 ESV. 2. Strongs G1127, gregoreo, Blue Letter Bible. 3. 1 Peter Ch 5v7-8 ESV.

48. STAY AWAKE - REMAIN VIGILANT.

1. 1 Peter Ch 5v8 NKJV. 2. Romans Ch 8v28 KJV. 3. Proverbs 16v19 NKJV. 4. Luke Ch 22v39-46 ESV.

49. STAY AWAKE - REMAIN FOCUSED.

1. Matthew Ch 11v3 ESV. 2. Psalm 84v10 NIV.

50. LOCKDOWN.

1. John Ch 20v19 ESV. 2. Ecclesiastes Ch 1v9 ESV. 3. 1 Corinthians Ch 15v6 ESV.

About the Author

Born in Northumberland, North East England, just a stone's throw from Hadrians' Wall, a fortification built by the Romans to mark the edge of their empire, which stretches across the breadth of England from the North Sea to the Irish Sea and separates Scotland from England. His parents relocated from the North East to Blackpool, a west coast seaside town where he spent all his formative years up to age 18. It was here as a 17yr old that he met Gail, one day after her 17th birthday. Two years later they married.

Mike and his wife Gail, gave their lives to the Lord at 30yrs of age, at this time they had been married for 11yrs. They have had many exciting adventures with the Lord and have repeatedly experienced God's goodness. In healing, provision, guidance and His loving support, not always how they had expected it.

Mike and Gail have now been married for over 40yrs, their two grown-up, adult children are married and they are now the proud grandparents of four grandchildren.

Mike and Gail currently live near the Solway Firth in South West Scotland, along with their daughter Gemma, her husband Tim and their two grandsons Joe and Ben. They are a family of creative Artisans, working with wood, paintings and soap-making. Mike believes that as we are made in the image of God, who is The Creator, we all have that creative desire within and the process of hands-on creativity brings peace to our hearts and minds and will lead us into healing. Mike and his family are currently actively seeking the Lord for whole healing for Gail.

Printed in the United States
by Baker & Taylor Publisher Services